# Transition Elements

**David Acaster**

**Series editor:** Brian Ratcliff

**CAMBRIDGE**
UNIVERSITY PRESS

PUBLISHED BY THE PRESS SYNDICATE OF THE UNIVERSITY OF CAMBRIDGE
The Pitt Building, Trumpington Street, Cambridge, United Kingdom

CAMBRIDGE UNIVERSITY PRESS
The Edinburgh Building, Cambridge CB2 2RU, UK
40 West 20th Street, New York, NY 10011-4211, USA
10 Stamford Road, Oakleigh, VIC 3166, Australia
Ruiz de Alarcón 13, 28014 Madrid, Spain
Dock House, The Waterfront, Cape Town 8001, South Africa

http://www.cambridge.org

© Cambridge University Press 2001

First published 2001

Printed in the United Kingdom at the University Press, Cambridge

*Typeface* Swift          *System*  QuarkXPress®

*A catalogue record for this book is available from the British Library*

ISBN 0 521 79752 7 paperback

Produced by Gecko Ltd, Bicester, Oxon

Front cover photograph: Coils of wire, Images Colour Library

# Contents

Acknowledgements    ii

Introduction    iv

## 1 The transition elements    1
What defines a transition element?    2
Oxidation and reduction    2
Which oxidation state forms in a reaction?    4

## 2 Electrode potentials    6
Electrode potentials    6
Standard electrode potentials    7
Measuring a standard electrode potential    8
The meaning of $E^{\ominus}$ values    11
Using $E^{\ominus}$ values to predict cell voltages    12
Using $E^{\ominus}$ values to predict whether or not
    a reaction will occur    13
The chemical reaction taking place in
    an electrochemical cell    16
Limitations of the standard electrode
    potential approach    16
Reaction rate has a role to play too    18
Using cell voltage to predict whether or not a
    reaction will occur – alternative approach    20

## 3 Ligands and complexes    22
Transition metal ions form complex ions    22
The shapes of complex ions    23
Stereoisomerism in transition metal complexes    24

## 4 Colour    29
Why are things coloured?    29
Why are many compounds not coloured?    32
Ligand substitution    34
The spectra of transition metal complexes    35

## 5 Case studies of four metals    39
Vanadium    39
Chromium    41
Cobalt    43
Copper    44

## Appendix
$E^{\ominus}$ data    50

Answers to self-assessment questions    51

Glossary    57

Index    59

# Introduction

## Cambridge Advanced Sciences

The *Cambridge Advanced Sciences* series has been developed to meet the demands of all the new AS and A level science examinations. In particular, it has been endorsed by OCR as providing complete coverage of their specifications. The AS material is presented as a single text for each of biology, chemistry and physics. Material for the A2 year comprises six books in each subject: one of core material and one for each option. Some material has been drawn from the existing *Cambridge Modular Sciences* books; however, many parts are entirely new.

During the development of this series, the opportunity has been taken to improve the design, and a complete and thorough new writing and editing process has been applied. Much more material is now presented in colour. Although the existing *Cambridge Modular Sciences* texts do cover most of the new specifications, the *Cambridge Advanced Sciences* books cover every OCR learning objective in detail. They are the key to success in the new AS and A level examinations.

OCR is one of the three unitary awarding bodies offering the full range of academic and vocational qualifications in the UK. For full details of the new specifications, please contact OCR:

OCR, 1 Hills Rd, Cambridge CB1 2EU
Tel: 01223 553311

### The presentation of units

You will find that the books in this series use a bracketed convention in the presentation of units within tables and on graph axes. For example, ionisation energies of $1000\,kJ\,mol^{-1}$ and $2000\,kJ\,mol^{-1}$ will be represented in this way:

| Measurement | Ionisation energy $(kJ\,mol^{-1})$ |
|---|---|
| 1 | 1000 |
| 2 | 2000 |

OCR examination papers use the solidus as a convention, thus:

| Measurement | Ionisation energy / $kJ\,mol^{-1}$ |
|---|---|
| 1 | 1000 |
| 2 | 2000 |

Any numbers appearing in brackets with the units, for example $(10^{-5}\,mol\,dm^{-3}\,s^{-1})$, should be treated in exactly the same way as when preceded by the solidus, $/10^{-5}\,mol\,dm^{-3}\,s^{-1}$.

## Transition Elements

*Transition elements* is all that is needed to cover the A2 chemistry option module of the same name. It is a brand new text which has been written specifically with the new OCR specification in mind. At the end of the book you will find a glossary of terms linked to the index, and answers to self-assessment questions.

### Acknowledgements

1.1, Robert Harding Picture Library; 1.2, 1.3, 1.4, 2.1, 2.2a, b, c, d, e, f, 2.15, 2.16, 2.18, 3.9, 4.4, 4.12, 5.1b, c, d, e, 5.4, 5.5, 5.6a, b, 5.8, 5.10, 5.11, 5.12, 5.13, 5.16a, b, c, d, e, f, Andrew Lambert; 1.5, Michael Holford; 1.6, Science & Society Picture Library; 1.7, Hugh Turvey/Science Photo Library; 1.8, Charles D. Winters/Science Photo Library; 4.1, Hank Morgan/ Science Photo Library; 4.2, John Chumack/Science Photo Library; 4.3b, © Zefa-Jaemsen/Powerstock/ Zefa; 4.10, DIY Photo Library; 5.1a, Science & Society Picture Library; 5.3, John Cole/Impact Photos; 5.7, Car Photo Library; 5.9, Michael Holford; 5.14, Popperfoto; 5.15, John Walmsley

Picture research: Maureen Cowdroy

With special thanks to the late Andrew Lambert and his family. The publisher is extremely grateful for the contribution Andrew made to so many of its books including this one, which was one of Andrew's final projects. He will be greatly missed.

# CHAPTER 1

# The transition elements

## By the end of this chapter you should be able to:

1 define a *transition element*;

2 calculate the *oxidation state* of each element in a compound;

3 understand *oxidation* and *reduction* in terms of electron transfer and change in oxidation state (oxidation number).

The **transition elements** are also called the transition metals. These metals are *very* useful! The photographs on this page illustrate one use of each element from titanium to copper .

● **Figure 1.1** Concorde is made of titanium alloy.

● **Figure 1.2** These jigsaw blades are made of vanadium.

● **Figure 1.3** The chromium used to plate parts of this bike looks good and won't rust.

● **Figure 1.4** Manganese alloy wire is used to make this laboratory rheostat and other resistors. Its resistance stays remarkably constant despite any temperature changes.

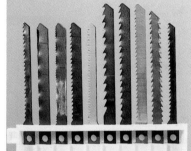

● **Figure 1.5** The Iron Age replaced the Bronze Age because an iron sword like this one was stronger than its bronze equivalent.

● **Figure 1.6** Cobalt is one of the key ingredients in this permanent magnet from a 1930's telephone.

● **Figure 1.7** The heating wires in this toaster are 80% nickel; they can operate at very high temperatures without burning out.

● **Figure 1.8** Copper's electrical conductivity per unit volume is higher than that of any other metal except silver.

# What defines a transition element?

In the Periodic Table the transition elements are found in a block that lies like a bridge from the s-block on the left to the p-block on the right. This block is called the d-block. The d-block begins with element 21, scandium, and its first row ends with element 30, zinc. Not all d-block elements are transition elements. A transition element is defined as an element that forms at least one ion with a partially filled d subshell. Scandium and zinc do not do this. This book will concentrate on the chemistry of the eight elements from titanium to copper. For our purposes, these are the transition elements. See *Chemistry 2*, chapter 11, for information on the electronic configurations of the transition elements.

## SAQ 1.1

The electronic configuration of scandium is [Ar] $3d^1 4s^2$, where [Ar] is $1s^2 2s^2 2p^6 3s^2 3p^6$. What is the electronic configuration of:

**a** zinc     **b** chromium     **c** iron?

## SAQ 1.2

The only ion formed by scandium is $Sc^{3+}$. The only ion formed by zinc is $Zn^{2+}$. Explain why scandium and zinc are not considered to be transition elements by referring to the electronic configurations of these two ions.

## SAQ 1.3

Titanium forms three different ions: $Ti^{2+}$, $Ti^{3+}$ and $Ti^{4+}$. Explain why titanium is considered to be a transition element by referring to the electronic configurations of these three ions.

# Oxidation and reduction

You will recall from *Chemistry 1*, chapter 5, and *Chemistry 2*, chapter 11, that the number of electrons gained or lost by each atom of an element in forming a compound is called its **oxidation state** in that compound. Electrons gained are shown by a negative oxidation state; electrons lost are shown by a positive oxidation state.

For example, when titanium burns in oxygen to form an oxide the titanium atoms each lose four electrons, so titanium has an oxidation state of +4 in this compound. The oxygen atoms each gain two electrons, so oxygen has an oxidation state of −2. The oxide formed is $TiO_2$ and is called titanium(IV) oxide.

> Oxidation states are usually written as Roman numerals when naming compounds. Oxidised states are given positive numbers, e.g. +VI. Reduced states are given negative numbers, e.g. −II.

Electrons may also be gained and lost in the reactions of compounds themselves.
- If a species (i.e. an atom or an ion in a compound) loses electrons in a reaction it is being **oxidised**.
- If a species gains electrons in a reaction it is being **reduced**.

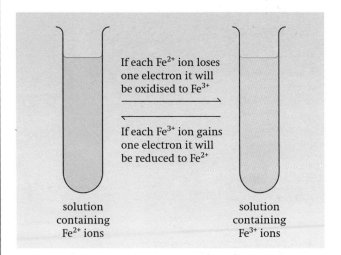

If each $Fe^{2+}$ ion loses one electron it will be oxidised to $Fe^{3+}$

If each $Fe^{3+}$ ion gains one electron it will be reduced to $Fe^{2+}$

solution containing $Fe^{2+}$ ions

solution containing $Fe^{3+}$ ions

● **Figure 1.9**

Reduction rarely happens to the ions of s-block elements; any reactions of a compound containing $Na^+$ ions will almost always give a product containing $Na^+$ ions – the oxidation state of sodium is +1 before and after the reaction.

Iron, however, forms compounds in the +2 state, containing the $Fe^{2+}$ ion, and in the +3 state, containing the $Fe^{3+}$ ion. During a reaction of a compound containing $Fe^{2+}$ ions each $Fe^{2+}$ ion may lose one electron, giving a product containing $Fe^{3+}$ ions.

## Working out oxidation states

There are rules for determining the values of oxidation states.

1 The oxidation state of uncombined elements (that is, elements not in compounds) is always zero. For example, each atom in Co(s), Fe(s) or Cu(s) has an oxidation state of zero.

2 For a monatomic ion, the oxidation state of the element is simply the same as the charge on the ion. For example:

| ion | $Fe^{2+}$ | $Fe^{3+}$ | $Cl^-$ | $O^{2-}$ |
|---|---|---|---|---|
| oxidation state | +2 | +3 | −1 | −2 |

3 The oxidation state of oxygen in compounds is −2.

4 The sum of all the oxidation states in a neutral compound is zero. For example, the sum of all the oxidation states in $FeCl_3$ is zero $(+3 + 3(−1) = 0)$.

5 The sum of all the oxidation states in an ion equals the overall charge. For example, the sum of all the oxidation states in $VO^{2+}$ is +2, $(+4 + −2 = +2)$.

(See also *Chemistry 1*, chapter 5, and *Chemistry 2*, chapter 11.)

### *Example 1*

What are the oxidation states of copper and chlorine in CuCl and $CuCl_2$?

Rules 2 and 4 above must be used here.

■ The oxidation state of chlorine in each compound is −1 as it exists as negative ions with a single minus charge (Rule 2).

■ In CuCl the oxidation state of copper is +1 to balance the single minus charge from the chloride ion in a neutral compound (Rule 4).

■ In $CuCl_2$ the oxidation state of copper is +2 to balance the two lots of single minus charges from two chloride ions in a neutral compound (Rule 4).

### *Example 2*

What is the oxidation state of vanadium in the vanadate ion $VO_2^+$?

Rules 3 and 5 above must be used here, since $VO_2^+$ is a compound ion.

■ The vanadate ion $VO_2^+$ has a single positive charge, so the sum of the oxidation states of vanadium and two oxygens must be +1 (Rule 5).

■ The two oxygens in this ion each have an oxidation state of −2 (Rule 3).

■ The oxidation state of the vanadium must be +5, since $+5 + (−2) + (−2) = +1$.

■ The $VO_2^+$ ion is therefore known as vanadate(v), spoken as 'vanadate five'.

All transition elements may be found in a variety of oxidation states in their compounds. An understanding of oxidation and reduction is therefore central to an understanding of the chemistry of the transition elements.

### Oxidation and reduction

Remember – OIL RIG

■ **Oxidation Is Loss** of electrons (OIL).

■ **Reduction Is Gain** of electrons (RIG).

A species that has been oxidised will have a higher oxidation state after the reaction than before. A species has been reduced if its oxidation state after the reaction is lower than before.

A reactant that causes another reactant to be oxidised in a reaction is called an **oxidising agent**. For example, a substance that reacts with an $Fe^{2+}$ compound giving an $Fe^{3+}$ compound as a product is an oxidising agent. The oxidising agent itself is reduced in the reaction.

A reactant that causes another reactant to be reduced in a reaction is likewise called a **reducing agent**. For example, a substance that reacts with an $Fe^{3+}$ compound giving an $Fe^{2+}$ compound as a product is a reducing agent. The reducing agent itself is oxidised in the reaction.

## SAQ 1.4

In the chemical reaction:

$Cu^{2+}Cl^-_2 + Fe \rightarrow Fe^{2+}Cl^-_2 + Cu$

**a** which species gains electrons and is therefore reduced?
**b** which species loses electrons and is therefore oxidised?
**c** which species is neither oxidised nor reduced?
**d** which species is the oxidising agent?
**e** which species is the reducing agent?

## SAQ 1.5

What is the oxidation state of chromium in compounds that contain the following ions?
**a** $CrO_4^{2-}$          **c** $Cr^{3+}$
**b** $Cr^{2+}$          **d** $Cr_2O_7^{2-}$

## SAQ 1.6

What is the oxidation state of manganese in the following compounds?
**a** $MnO_2$          **c** Mn          **e** $MnCl_3$
**b** $K_2MnO_4$          **d** $KMnO_4$          **f** $MnCl_2$

# Which oxidation state forms in a reaction?

When an s-block element such as magnesium reacts with an oxidising agent such as dilute acid, the outcome is always the same – a compound containing $Mg^{2+}$ ions. For example:

$Mg + 2HCl \rightarrow MgCl_2 + H_2$

Magnesium is *not* a transition element, it only forms compounds in the +2 oxidation state, so the outcome is quite easy to predict.

However, when a transition element reacts with an oxidising agent there will, on occasions, seem to be more than one possible outcome. For example, when iron metal reacts with dilute hydrochloric acid there are two possible outcomes:

$Fe + 2HCl \rightarrow FeCl_2 + H_2$

or

$2Fe + 6HCl \rightarrow 2FeCl_3 + 3H_2$

Which is the correct equation?

Only one of these two reactions actually takes place, but due to the fact that iron forms stable compounds in the +2 oxidation state *and* the +3 oxidation state, either *might* be correct.

Examining the oxidation states of all species in these equations shows that the oxidising agent in each case is $H^+$ ions. $H^+$ ions are reduced to hydrogen gas so the $H^+$ ions must be oxidising another species.

We can therefore restate the question as: Is $H^+$ a strong enough oxidising agent to oxidise iron to $Fe^{3+}$ ions (the second equation) or only as far as $Fe^{2+}$ ions (the first equation)? The answer to this question can be found experimentally, but it can also be predicted using an understanding of standard electrode potentials, and that will be the subject of the next chapter of this book.

## SAQ 1.7

For both of the two equations above, give the oxidation number of each species before and after the reaction and identify the reducing agent.

# SUMMARY

- A transition element is an element that forms at least one compound with a partly filled d subshell.

- The oxidation state (oxidation number) of each element in a compound can be calculated by following simple rules.

- An element is oxidised in a chemical reaction if its oxidation state increases; an element is reduced in a chemical reaction if its oxidation state decreases.

- An oxidising agent causes another substance in a reaction to be oxidised. A reducing agent causes another substance in a reaction to be reduced.

# Questions

1  Give the electronic configuration of:
   a  a vanadium atom
   b  a $V^{2+}$ ion
   c  a $V^{3+}$ ion.

2  Explain why the existence of compounds containing $V^{2+}$ ions proves that vanadium is a transition element.

3  Consider the following reactions involving chromium compounds.

|   | Reactant | Product |
|---|----------|---------|
| A | $K_2Cr_2O_7$ | $CrCl_3$ |
| B | $K_2Cr_2O_7$ | $K_2CrO_4$ |
| C | $CrCl_3$ | $CrCl_2$ |
| D | $Cr_2O_3$ | $CrCl_3$ |
| E | $Cr_2O_3$ | $K_2Cr_2O_7$ |

   a  In which of these reactions is chromium oxidised?
   b  In which of these reactions is chromium reduced?
   c  In which of these reactions is chromium neither oxidised nor reduced?
   d  In which of these reactions must the stated reactant be treated with an oxidising agent?
   e  In which of these reactions must the stated reactant be treated with a reducing agent?

4  Rutile is a titanium ore containing $TiO_2$. Titanium metal is obtained from it by first producing $TiCl_4$ from the $TiO_2$. The $TiCl_4$ is then heated with a metal such as magnesium or sodium to give titanium metal.
   a  What is the oxidation state of titanium in:
      (i)  $TiO_2$
      (ii)  $TiCl_4$
      (iii)  titanium metal?
   b  Write balanced chemical equations for the reaction of $TiCl_4$ with:
      (i)  magnesium
      (ii)  sodium.
   c  For each reaction in part b, identify:
      (i)  the species oxidised
      (ii)  the species reduced
      (iii)  the oxidising agent
      (iv)  the reducing agent.

5  This question is about the following vanadium compounds:
   $VCl_2$
   $VOCl_2$
   $NH_4VO_3$
   $VCl_3$
   $VO_2Cl$
   a  What is the oxidation state of vanadium in each compound? Which two compounds have vanadium in the same oxidation state?
   b  Give the electronic configuration of vanadium in $VCl_3$ and explain why vanadium is considered to be a transition element.
   c  If $VCl_3$ were reduced in a chemical reaction which of the other compounds in this question *might* be the product?

# CHAPTER 2

# Electrode potentials

## By the end of this chapter you should be able to:

1 define the term *standard electrode (redox) potential*, and be familiar with the symbol for standard electrode potential, which is $E^{\ominus}$;

2 describe how a *standard reference electrode* is used to measure the standard electrode potential of a metal or a non-metal in contact with its ions in aqueous solution;

3 describe how a standard reference electrode is used to measure the standard electrode potential of a system containing ions of the same element in different oxidation states;

4 calculate a *standard cell potential* using standard electrode potential data;

5 use standard cell potentials to predict whether or not a reaction will occur spontaneously;

6 recognise that standard cell potentials refer to particular concentrations, and that changing these concentrations will affect the accuracy of any predictions;

7 recognise that standard cell potential data cannot tell you whether or not a spontaneous reaction occurs at a suitable rate – it may be too slow.

## Electrode potentials

Reduction reactions involve a substance gaining electrons. For example, metal ions can gain electrons in reactions and be reduced to metals, e.g.

$$Cu^{2+} + 2e^- \rightleftharpoons Cu$$

$$V^{2+} + 2e^- \rightleftharpoons V$$

Equations of this sort are called **half-equations**.

Some metals ions, such as $Cu^{2+}$ ions, are very easy to reduce like this, while other metal ions, such as $V^{2+}$ ions, are much harder. Fortunately for us, we can measure the ease with which the reduction takes place – we are not restricted to simple comparative words like 'easier' and 'harder'. The measured value is called the **electrode potential** for this reduction. It is measured in volts (V) and is a numerical indication of how favourable (or 'easy') the reduction is. Note that it is a convention that electrode potentials refer to the reduction reaction.

■ If the electrode potential is a more positive voltage the ion on the left is comparatively easy to reduce. For

$$Cu^{2+} + 2e^- \rightleftharpoons Cu$$

the voltage is +0.34 V.

■ If the electrode potential is a more negative voltage the ion on the left is comparatively hard to reduce. For

$$V^{2+} + 2e^- \rightleftharpoons V$$

the voltage is −1.20 V.

Therefore, it is easier to reduce $Cu^{2+}$ ions to Cu atoms than it is to reduce $V^{2+}$ ions to V atoms.

Remember the convention that electrode potentials refer to reduction reactions. In the reaction above, −1.20 V refers to

$$V^{2+} + 2e^- \rightleftharpoons V$$

the reduction reaction, and not to

$$V \rightleftharpoons V^{2+} + 2e^-$$

which would be an oxidation.

## How is the voltage for $Cu^{2+} + 2e^- \rightleftharpoons Cu$ measured?

In order to measure the electrode potential in volts for this reduction, a rod of pure copper must be placed in a $1.00 \, mol \, dm^{-3}$ solution of $Cu^{2+}$ ions (e.g. copper(II) sulphate solution) at a temperature of 25 °C (298 K) (*figure 2.1*). Unfortunately, the electrode potential cannot be measured using this set-up alone. The $Cu^{2+}$/Cu system described here cannot gain or lose electrons unless it is connected electrically to a similar system that will either provide or take up these electrons. The $Cu^{2+}$/Cu system is called a **half-cell**.

In order to work as required and give us a measure of how easy it is to reduce $Cu^{2+}$ ions to Cu atoms this half-cell *must* be connected to another half-cell. Connecting two half-cells together makes an **electrochemical cell**. An electrochemical cell has a voltage that can be measured and can be used to produce electrical energy and light a bulb. The sort of batteries that go in torches are simply cleverly packaged electrochemical cells. For convenience their wet ingredients are included in paste form, so they are called 'dry cells'.

## Standard electrode potentials

If the $Cu^{2+}$/Cu half-cell described above is connected electrically to another half-cell then a complete electrochemical cell has been created and the cell voltage can be measured. If the other half-cell consists of a $1.00 \, mol \, dm^{-3}$ solution of $H^+$ ions in contact with hydrogen gas at 1 atmosphere pressure, all at a temperature of 298 K, then the voltage measured is called the **standard electrode potential** for the reaction

$$Cu^{2+} + 2e^- \rightleftharpoons Cu$$

The $H^+/H_2$ half-cell is called a **standard hydrogen electrode**.

A second half-cell of some kind is used because it is impossible to measure the voltage of the $Cu^{2+}$/Cu half-cell on its own. A standard hydrogen electrode in particular is used as the second half-cell when measuring standard electrode potentials because this is what chemists have agreed upon. There is nothing particularly special about the $H^+/H_2$ half-cell, although the fact that it was chosen in this way gives it a special place in electrochemistry.

This seems like quite a fiddly way to collect data, but the data collected is *very* useful.

Look again at your answers to SAQ 1.6 (page 4). Manganese can form stable compounds in *five* different oxidation states (*figure 2.2*). Using standard electrode potential data it is possible to predict accurately which oxidation state of manganese forms in any particular reaction.

copper rod

$Cu^{2+}$, 1 mol dm$^{-3}$
298 K

● **Figure 2.1** The $Cu^{2+}$/Cu half-cell.

**a** Manganese(0), the metal as an element.    **b** Manganese(II), as a $Mn^{2+}$ solution.    **c** Manganese(III), as a $Mn^{3+}$ solution.    **d** Manganese(IV), as solid $MnO_2$.    **e** Manganese(VI), as the $MnO_4^{2-}$ ion.    **f** Manganese(VII), as the $MnO_4^-$ ion.

**Figure 2.2** The various oxidation states of manganese.

## The standard hydrogen electrode

A standard hydrogen electrode is shown in *figure 2.3*. Hydrogen gas is introduced into the standard hydrogen electrode at the top and bubbles out slowly from a hole in the glass bell. The platinum electrode allows electrical contact to be made. Platinum ensures good contact between $H^+$ ions and $H_2$ molecules so that electrode reactions occur quickly, but being an inert metal it does not take part in any reactions itself. The platinum electrode needs to be coated with finely divided platinum (known as platinum black).

The two possible electrode reactions here are

$$H^+ + e^- \rightarrow \tfrac{1}{2}H_2$$

if the other half-cell gives electrons to the standard hydrogen electrode, or

$$\tfrac{1}{2}H_2 \rightarrow H^+ + e^-$$

if the standard hydrogen electrode gives electrons to the other half-cell.

The standard hydrogen electrode is used as a **standard reference electrode** – if it is connected to another half-cell then the electrode potential of the other half-cell can be measured *relative* to the voltage of the standard hydrogen electrode. It is a lot like measuring the height of a mountain – the height is always given relative to sea level.

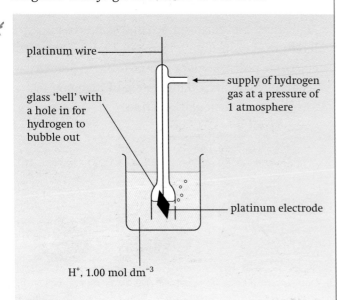

● **Figure 2.3** The standard hydrogen electrode.

platinum wire

glass 'bell' with a hole in for hydrogen to bubble out

supply of hydrogen gas at a pressure of 1 atmosphere

platinum electrode

$H^+$, 1.00 mol dm$^{-3}$

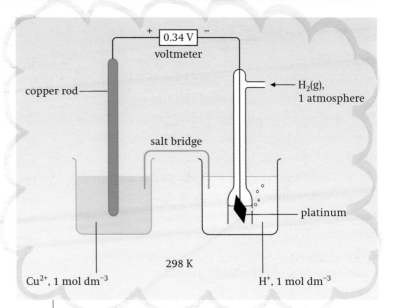

0.34 V
voltmeter

copper rod

$H_2$(g), 1 atmosphere

salt bridge

platinum

298 K

Cu$^{2+}$, 1 mol dm$^{-3}$

H$^+$, 1 mol dm$^{-3}$

● **Figure 2.4** Measuring the standard electrode potential of a $Cu^{2+}/Cu$ half-cell.

## Measuring a standard electrode potential

If all concentrations are $1.00\,\text{mol}\,\text{dm}^{-3}$, if the temperature is 298 K and if the pressures of any gases used are 1 atmosphere, then these conditions are called **standard conditions**. If an electrochemical cell is made up under standard conditions, using a standard hydrogen electrode as one half-cell and the half-cell under investigation as the second half-cell, then the voltage measured is the standard electrode potential of the half-cell under investigation (*figure 2.4*).

The **salt bridge** in *figure 2.4* is there to complete the electric circuit. A simple salt bridge can be made by soaking a piece of filter paper in potassium nitrate solution. The salt bridge completes the electric circuit by allowing movement of ions between the two half-cells. It does not allow the movement of electrons – these flow via the external circuit only.

The voltage of this electrochemical cell is 0.34 V, with the copper half-cell as the positive terminal and the hydrogen half-cell as the negative terminal. Since conditions are standard and the other half-cell is a standard hydrogen electrode, this means that +0.34 V is the standard electrode potential for the half-cell reaction

$$Cu^{2+} + 2e^- \rightleftharpoons Cu$$

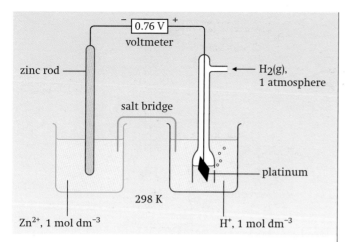

● **Figure 2.5** Measuring the standard electrode potential of a $Zn^{2+}/Zn$ half-cell.

This value of +0.34 V gives a numerical indication of the tendency of $Cu^{2+}$ ions to receive electrons, and of Cu atoms to lose electrons. It can be used to predict with accuracy which reactions $Cu^{2+}$ ions and Cu atoms will take part in.

The voltage of the electrochemical cell shown in *figure 2.5* is 0.76 V, with the zinc half-cell as the negative terminal and the hydrogen half-cell as the positive terminal. Since conditions are standard and the other half-cell is a standard hydrogen electrode, this means that −0.76 V is the standard electrode potential for the half-cell reaction

$$Zn^{2+} + 2e^- \rightleftharpoons Zn$$

(Remember the convention that half-equations are written as reductions.) This value of −0.76 V gives a numerical value of the tendency of $Zn^{2+}$ ions to receive electrons, and of Zn atoms to lose electrons. Since it is a more negative value than the value for $Cu^{2+}/Cu$ it means that $Zn^{2+}$ has a *lower* tendency to gain electrons than $Cu^{2+}$ has, and zinc has a *greater* tendency to lose electrons than copper has. This will be explained further in the section 'The meaning of $E^{\ominus}$ values' (page 11). The way in which standard electrode potential values can be used is explained further in the section 'Using $E^{\ominus}$ values to predict whether or not a reaction will occur' (page 13).

> The standard electrode potential for a half-cell reaction can therefore be defined as the voltage measured under standard conditions when the half-cell is incorporated into an electrochemical cell with the other half-cell being a standard hydrogen electrode.

The symbol for a standard electrode potential is $E^{\ominus}$, usually pronounced 'E nought' or 'E standard', with the $^{\ominus}$ sign representing standard conditions. We can therefore write:

$$Cu^{2+} + 2e^- \rightleftharpoons Cu; \qquad E^{\ominus} = +0.34\,V$$
$$Zn^{2+} + 2e^- \rightleftharpoons Zn; \qquad E^{\ominus} = -0.76\,V$$

## SAQ 2.1

Look at the electrochemical cells shown in *figure 2.6*.
a  Write equations for the half-cell reactions in the half-cells on the left of each diagram (i.e. *not* the standard hydrogen electrode). Write each equation as a reduction (gain of electrons), e.g.

$$Zn^{2+} + 2e^- \rightleftharpoons Zn$$

b  What are the standard electrode potentials for these half-cell reactions?
c  List all necessary conditions in each cell.

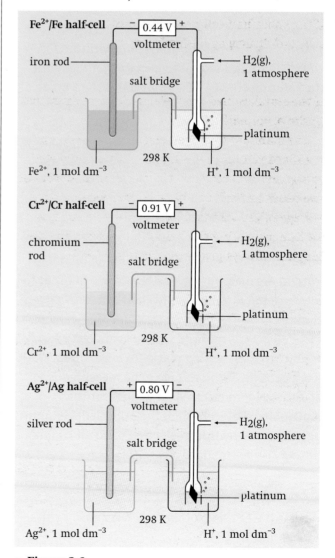

● **Figure 2.6**

The standard electrode potential for a half-cell reaction is the measured voltage of an electrochemical cell consisting of the half-cell and a standard hydrogen electrode. All conditions must be standard. The polarity of the half-cell within this electrochemical cell gives the sign of the standard electrode potential.

## Measuring standard electrode potentials involving two ions

We have considered how the standard electrode potential of a metal in contact with one of its ions can be measured. Standard electrode potentials can also be measured for reductions in which both the species involved are ions. For example:

$$Fe^{3+} + e^- \rightleftharpoons Fe^{2+}$$

The half-cell that is used here must contain *both* $Fe^{2+}$ ions and $Fe^{3+}$ ions, both at a concentration of $1.00 \, mol \, dm^{-3}$. A platinum wire or platinum foil electrode is used to make electrical contact with the solution. The $Fe^{3+}/Fe^{2+}$ half-cell is then made into an electrochemical cell with a standard hydrogen electrode as the other half-cell. The measured voltage, the $E^\ominus$ value, is +0.77 V (*figure 2.7*).

Some reductions involve several ionic species. For example:

$$MnO_4^- + 8H^+ + 5e^- \rightleftharpoons Mn^{2+} + 4H_2O$$

The inclusion of $H^+$ ions here means that acid conditions are necessary for the reduction of $MnO_4^-$ ions (manganate(VII) ions) to $Mn^{2+}$ ions. In order to measure the $E^\ominus$ value for this half-cell, the concentrations of $MnO_4^-$ ions, $H^+$ ions and $Mn^{2+}$ ions must all be $1.00 \, mol \, dm^{-3}$. Once again electrical contact is made with a platinum wire or platinum foil electrode. If the voltage to be measured is to be the standard electrode potential for the $MnO_4^-/Mn^{2+}$ half-cell, then the other half-cell must be a standard hydrogen electrode and all conditions must be standard (*figure 2.8*).

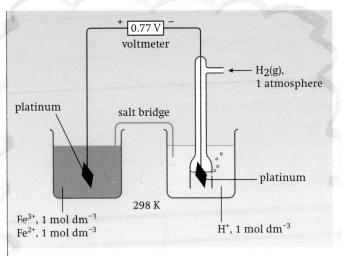

● **Figure 2.7** Measuring the standard electrode potential of an $Fe^{3+}/Fe^{2+}$ half-cell.

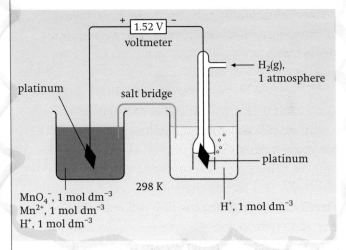

● **Figure 2.8** Measuring the standard electrode potential of an $MnO_4^-/Mn^{2+}$ half-cell.

### SAQ 2.3
What are standard conditions?

### SAQ 2.4
Why is platinum used in preference to other metals in half-cells where the reaction itself does not involve a metal element?

### SAQ 2.5
Show, with the aid of a diagram, how you would measure the $E^\ominus$ value for the half-cell shown by this equation:

$$VO^{2+} + 2H^+ + e^- \rightleftharpoons V^{3+} + H_2O$$

### SAQ 2.2
What is the $E^\ominus$ value for the half-cell shown by this equation?

$$MnO_4^- + 8H^+ + 5e^- \rightleftharpoons Mn^{2+} + 4H_2O$$

## Measuring standard electrode potentials involving non-metals

We can also measure the standard electrode potential for a non-metallic element in contact with a solution of its aqueous ions. As with measuring the standard electrode potential of two ions of the same element in different oxidation states, one difficulty here is how to make electrical contact. The answer again is to use a platinum wire.

The platinum wire must be in contact with both the element and the aqueous ions. The standard electrode potential is measured by connecting the half-cell to a standard hydrogen electrode and measuring the voltage produced under standard conditions.

The half-cell on the left of *figure 2.9* involves chlorine gas and chloride ions. The half-equation is therefore

$$\tfrac{1}{2}Cl_2 + e^- \rightleftharpoons Cl^-$$

The $E^\ominus$ value for this half-cell is +1.36 V.

You should note that the half-equation could also have been written

$$Cl_2 + 2e^- \rightleftharpoons 2Cl^-$$

The $E^\ominus$ value for this half-cell is still +1.36 V. The way in which you choose to balance the half-equation makes no difference to the tendency for the element chlorine to gain electrons!

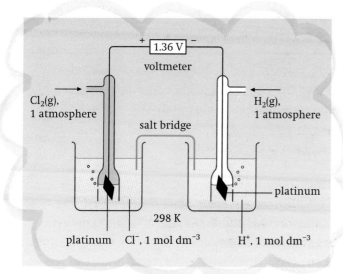

● **Figure 2.9** Measuring the standard electrode potential of a $Cl_2/Cl^-$ half-cell.

**SAQ 2.6**

Look at the diagram in *figure 2.10* and write a half-equation for the half-cell on the left. What is the $E^\ominus$ value for this half-cell?

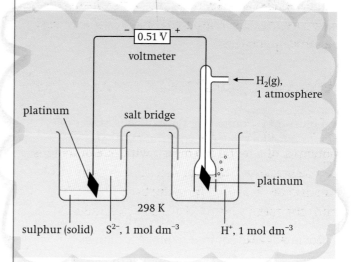

● **Figure 2.10** Measuring the standard electrode potential of an $S/S^{2-}$ half-cell.

**SAQ 2.7**

Draw a diagram to show how you would measure the standard electrode potential for the half-cell

$$\tfrac{1}{2}I_2 + e^- \rightleftharpoons I^-$$

Include the actual $E^\ominus$ value of +0.54 V on your diagram.

If a cell is made using two identical half-cells, the voltage measured is always zero volts. This means that measuring the $E^\ominus$ for the half-cell

$$H^+ + e^- \rightleftharpoons \tfrac{1}{2}H_2$$

gives a value of 0.00 V. This value arises because of our choice of a standard hydrogen electrode as reference electrode, but it is still a relevant and useful piece of data.

# The meaning of $E^\ominus$ values

The previous section on measuring $E^\ominus$ values has explained how standard electrode potentials are measured using a half-cell, a standard hydrogen electrode, a salt bridge and a voltmeter. This section begins to explain how useful this data is to us.

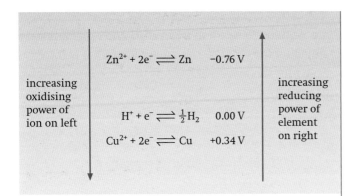

$$Zn^{2+} + 2e^- \rightleftharpoons Zn \quad -0.76\,V$$

increasing oxidising power of ion on left

$$H^+ + e^- \rightleftharpoons \tfrac{1}{2}H_2 \quad 0.00\,V$$

$$Cu^{2+} + 2e^- \rightleftharpoons Cu \quad +0.34\,V$$

increasing reducing power of element on right

● **Figure 2.11** Comparing the oxidising power of ions and the reducing power of elements.

$E^\ominus$ values give us a measure of how easy a reduction or oxidation is to carry out. (In this context 'easy' refers to the strength of oxidising or reducing agent required to make a change happen. If a species is 'easy' to oxidise it can be oxidised by a weaker oxidising agent.) This can be summarised in three ways.

■ The more positive a value of $E^\ominus$ is, the greater the tendency for this half-equation to proceed in a forward direction.

■ The more positive the value of $E^\ominus$, the easier it is to reduce the species on the left of the half-equation.

■ The less positive the value of $E^\ominus$, the easier it is to oxidise the species on the right of the half-equation.

Consider the following two half-equations as examples:

$$Cu^{2+} + 2e^- \rightleftharpoons Cu; \qquad E^\ominus = +0.34\,V$$
$$Zn^{2+} + 2e^- \rightleftharpoons Zn; \qquad E^\ominus = -0.76\,V$$

■ Comparing the two half-equations, $Cu^{2+}/Cu$ has a greater tendency to proceed in the forward direction, as its $E^\ominus$ value is more positive. $Zn^{2+}/Zn$ has a greater tendency to proceed in the backward direction, as its $E^\ominus$ value is more negative (figure 2.11).

■ The $Cu^{2+}/Cu$ half-equation has the more positive $E^\ominus$ value, so $Cu^{2+}$ is easier to reduce to Cu than $Zn^{2+}$ is to Zn. $Zn^{2+}$ ions can be reduced to Zn metal, but this requires a stronger reducing agent, with a more negative $E^\ominus$ value than the $E^\ominus$ value for $Zn^{2+}/Zn$.

■ The $Zn^{2+}/Zn$ half-equation has the less positive $E^\ominus$ value, so Zn is easier to oxidise to $Zn^{2+}$ than

Cu is to $Cu^{2+}$. Cu metal *can* be oxidised to $Cu^{2+}$ ions, but it requires a stronger oxidising agent, with a more positive $E^\ominus$ value than the $E^\ominus$ value for $Cu^{2+}/Cu$.

## SAQ 2.8

Use the $E^\ominus$ data from page 50 to answer this question.

**a** Of the ions $Ag^+$, $Cr^{2+}$ and $Fe^{2+}$, which one needs the strongest reducing agent to reduce it to uncharged metal atoms?

**b** Of the atoms Ag, Cr and Fe, which one needs the strongest oxidising agent to oxidise it to an ion?

# Using $E^\ominus$ values to predict cell voltages

You have learnt how the $E^\ominus$ value of a half-cell can be measured and what the $E^\ominus$ value can tell us about how easy it is to oxidise or reduce a particular species. $E^\ominus$ values can also be used to calculate the voltage of an electrochemical cell made of two half-cells, and to predict whether or not a particular reaction occurs. This section deals with cell voltages.

To recap, if an electrochemical cell is made using two half-cells, standard conditions and a salt bridge, and if one of the half-cells is a standard hydrogen electrode then the voltage measured is the standard electrode potential of the other half-cell. However, if two half-cells are used, neither of which is a standard hydrogen electrode, then the voltage measured will be the *difference* in the $E^\ominus$ values of the two half-cells.

For the electrochemical cell shown in *figure 2.12*, the standard electrode potentials are:

$$Ag^+ + e^- \rightleftharpoons Ag; \qquad E^\ominus = +0.80\,V$$
$$Zn^{2+} + 2e^- \rightleftharpoons Zn; \qquad E^\ominus = -0.76\,V$$

The difference between +0.80 V and −0.76 V is +1.56 V (+0.80 − (−0.76) = +1.56) (*figure 2.13*). The voltage of this cell is therefore +1.56 V. Since the standard electrode potential of the $Ag^+/Ag$ half-cell is more positive, the $Ag^+/Ag$ half-cell will be the positive pole and the $Zn^{2+}/Zn$ half-cell will be the negative pole of the cell.

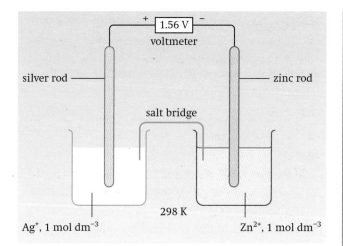

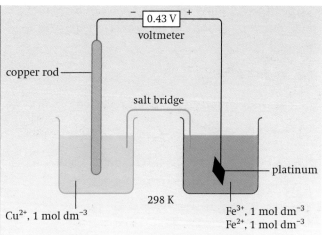

● **Figure 2.12** An $Ag^+/Ag$, $Zn^{2+}/Zn$ electrochemical cell.

● **Figure 2.14** A $Cu^{2+}/Cu$, $Fe^{3+}/Fe^{2+}$ electrochemical cell.

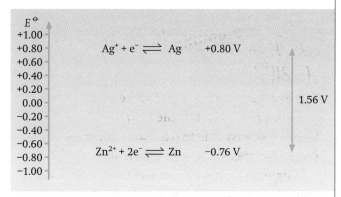

● **Figure 2.13** The difference between $+0.80\,V$ and $-0.76\,V$ is $+1.56\,V$.

For the electrochemical cell shown in *figure 2.14*, the standard electrode potentials are:

$$Fe^{3+} + e^- \rightleftharpoons Fe^{2+}; \qquad E^\ominus = +0.77\,V$$
$$Cu^{2+} + 2e^- \rightleftharpoons Cu; \qquad E^\ominus = +0.34\,V$$

The difference between $+0.77\,V$ and $+0.34\,V$ is $+0.43\,V$ ($+0.77 - (+0.34) = +0.43$). The voltage of this cell is therefore $+0.43\,V$. Since the standard electrode potential of the $Fe^{3+}/Fe^{2+}$ half-cell is more positive, the $Fe^{3+}/Fe^{2+}$ half-cell will be the positive pole, and the $Cu^{2+}/Cu$ half-cell will be the negative pole of the cell.

## SAQ 2.9

**a** Draw a diagram of an electrochemical cell consisting of a $Cr^{3+}/Cr$ half-cell and a $Cl_2/Cl^-$ half-cell.

**b** What will be the cell voltage?

**c** Which half-cell will be the positive pole?

All necessary $E^\ominus$ values can be found on page 50.

## SAQ 2.10

**a** Draw a diagram of an electrochemical cell consisting of a $Mn^{2+}/Mn$ half-cell and a $Pb^{2+}/Pb$ half-cell.

**b** What will be the cell voltage?

**c** Which half-cell will be the positive pole?

All necessary $E^\ominus$ values can be found on page 50.

# Using $E^\ominus$ values to predict whether or not a reaction will occur

An understanding of standard electrode potentials makes it possible to predict whether or not a particular oxidising agent can or cannot oxidise another named substance under standard conditions. It is also possible to predict whether or not a particular reducing agent can reduce another substance.

To find out whether or not a solution of $Cu^{2+}$ ions can oxidise zinc metal to $Zn^{2+}$ ions, first of all write down the half-equations with their standard electrode potential values:

$$Zn^{2+} + 2e^- \rightleftharpoons Zn; \qquad E^\ominus = -0.76\,V$$
$$Cu^{2+} + 2e^- \rightleftharpoons Cu; \qquad E^\ominus = +0.34\,V$$

The bottom half-equation has a more positive standard electrode potential value than the top one. This means that the bottom reaction can proceed in a forward direction (meaning $Cu^{2+}$ is reduced to copper) while the top reaction proceeds in a backward direction (meaning zinc is oxidised to $Zn^{2+}$). Therefore, $Cu^{2+}$ ions *can* oxidise zinc metal.

To write an equation for this reaction rewrite the two half-equations in the directions in which they will proceed:

$$Zn \rightarrow Zn^{2+} + 2e^-$$

(the zinc half-equation has been reversed)

$$Cu^{2+} + 2e^- \rightarrow Cu$$

(this half-equation has been left unchanged).
Adding the two half-equations gives:

$$Zn + Cu^{2+} + 2e^- \rightarrow Cu + Zn^{2+} + 2e^-$$

Cancelling the two electrons on each side gives:

$$Zn + Cu^{2+} \rightarrow Cu + Zn^{2+}$$

So, it is this reaction that takes place (*figure 2.15*) and not its opposite ($Zn^{2+} + Cu \rightarrow Cu^{2+} + Zn$). This may seem like a trivial example, involving a reaction you have been familiar with for some years, but it illustrates the predictive power of $E^\ominus$ values. Using $E^\ominus$ values enables you to predict whether or not a reaction takes place.

## Worked examples

### Can chlorine oxidise $Fe^{2+}$ ions to $Fe^{3+}$ ions?

First of all write down the half-equations with their standard electrode potential values:

$$Fe^{3+} + e^- \rightleftharpoons Fe^{2+}; \qquad\qquad E^\ominus = +0.77\,V$$
$$\tfrac{1}{2}Cl_2 + e^- \rightleftharpoons Cl^-; \qquad\qquad E^\ominus = +1.36\,V$$

The bottom half-equation, with its more positive standard electrode potential value, will proceed in a forward direction ($Cl_2$ is reduced to $Cl^-$ ions) while the top reaction proceeds in a backward direction ($Fe^{2+}$ is oxidised to $Fe^{3+}$). Therefore, chlorine *can* oxidise $Fe^{2+}$ ions. To write an equation for this reaction rewrite the two half-equations in the directions in which they will proceed:

$$\tfrac{1}{2}Cl_2 + e^- \rightarrow Cl^-$$
$$Fe^{2+} \rightarrow Fe^{3+} + e^-$$

Adding the two half-equations together and cancelling the electron on each side gives:

$$\tfrac{1}{2}Cl_2 + Fe^{2+} \rightarrow Cl^- + Fe^{3+}$$

### Can iodine oxidise $Fe^{2+}$ to $Fe^{3+}$?

The half-equations and $E^\ominus$ values are:

$$\tfrac{1}{2}I_2 + e^- \rightleftharpoons I^-; \qquad\qquad E^\ominus = +0.54\,V$$
$$Fe^{3+} + e^- \rightleftharpoons Fe^{2+}; \qquad\qquad E^\ominus = +0.77\,V$$

With a less positive $E^\ominus$ value the top reaction cannot proceed forward while the bottom reaction proceeds backward. Iodine *cannot* oxidise $Fe^{2+}$ to $Fe^{3+}$ under standard conditions.

> The half-cell that gains electrons is always the one with the more positive $E^\ominus$ value. The half-cell that supplies electrons is always the one with the more negative $E^\ominus$ value. Remember – positive attracts electrons; negative repels electrons.

● **Figure 2.15** As predicted by the $E^\ominus$ values, zinc reacts with $Cu^{2+}$ ions but copper does not react with $Zn^{2+}$ ions.

## SAQ 2.11

Although iodine cannot oxidise $Fe^{2+}$ to $Fe^{3+}$, the half-equations predict that another reaction involving iodide ions and iron in a particular oxidation state *is* possible. Write an equation for this reaction.

The half-equations in the worked examples above both involve one electron only. This will not always be the case.

When using this method to find out whether or not a solution of $Ag^+$ can oxidise chromium metal to $Cr^{3+}$ the silver half-equation involves one electron, but the chromium half-equation involves three. Writing a balanced ionic equation for the reaction, if it occurs, will involve balancing the number of electrons involved.

Starting as before with the half-equations:

$$Cr^{3+} + 3e^- \rightleftharpoons Cr; \qquad E^\ominus = -0.74\,V$$
$$Ag^+ + e^- \rightleftharpoons Ag; \qquad E^\ominus = +0.80\,V$$

The bottom half-equation, with its more positive standard electrode potential value, will proceed in a forward direction while the top reaction proceeds in a backward direction. $Ag^+$ *can* oxidise chromium metal to $Cr^{3+}$ ions. Rewriting the half-equations in the directions in which they will proceed gives:

$$Cr \rightarrow Cr^{3+} + 3e^-$$
$$Ag^+ + e^- \rightarrow Ag$$

Before adding these together, the same number of electrons must be involved in each half-equation. In this case that means three electrons, so the bottom equation must be multiplied by three:

$$Cr \rightarrow Cr^{3+} + 3e^-$$
$$3Ag^+ + 3e^- \rightarrow 3Ag$$

Adding now gives:

$$Cr + 3Ag^+ + 3e^- \rightarrow Cr^{3+} + 3e^- + 3Ag$$

Cancelling the electrons gives:

$$Cr + 3Ag^+ \rightarrow Cr^{3+} + 3Ag$$

The final equation, therefore, says that one chromium atom can be oxidised to a $Cr^{3+}$ ion by three $Ag^+$ ions, which in turn are reduced to three silver atoms.

## SAQ 2.12

Use the $E^\ominus$ data on page 50 to predict whether or not the following reactions occur. If a reaction does occur, write a balanced chemical equation for it.

**a** Can $MnO_4^-$ ions oxidise $Cl^-$ ions to chlorine in acid conditions?

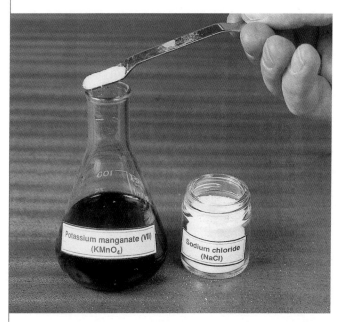

● **Figure 2.16** If the $KMnO_4(aq)$ is acidified, would it be safe to do this in an open lab or would chlorine gas be produced?

**b** Can $MnO_4^-$ ions oxidise $F^-$ ions to fluorine in acid conditions?
**c** Can $H^+$ ions oxidise $V^{2+}$ ions to $V^{3+}$ ions?
**d** Can $H^+$ ions oxidise $Fe^{2+}$ ions to $Fe^{3+}$ ions?

You now have the answer, from SAQ 2.12, part **d**, to the question in chapter 1, page 4: Is $H^+$ a strong enough oxidising agent to oxidise iron to $Fe^{3+}$ ions or only as far as $Fe^{2+}$ ions? It took some time to get here, because some detailed and subtle concepts have been involved, but if you have mastered the meaning and application of $E^\ominus$ values you now have a powerful tool for assessing whether or not a reaction occurs, and if it does occur which of several possible outcomes arises.

An alternative approach to this topic is given at the end of this chapter (pages 20 and 21).
*It is recommended that you choose only one of these two approaches in predicting whether or not a reaction occurs.*

# The chemical reaction taking place in an electrochemical cell

You will remember that an electrochemical cell is made of two half-cells joined by a salt bridge. When an electrochemical cell is working and producing a voltage, chemical energy is being converted into electrical energy. Therefore a chemical reaction is taking place, part of it in one half-cell and part of it in the other. When the reactants are used up in the cells that we put in torches etc , they stop working and we say they have run down or 'gone flat'.

The reaction that takes place is the one predicted by looking at the $E^{\ominus}$ values of the two half-cells. This reaction occurs just as successfully in the two separated half-cells as it does if the ingredients are put together in one beaker. The difference is that in the two separated half-cells the energy released by the reaction is in the form of electrical energy. When mixed in a beaker the reactants release this energy as heat.

In the example in *figure 2.17*, the half-equations are:

$$Ni^{2+} + 2e^- \rightleftharpoons Ni; \qquad\qquad E^{\ominus} = -0.25\,V$$
$$Fe^{3+} + e^- \rightleftharpoons Fe^{2+}; \qquad\qquad E^{\ominus} = +0.77\,V$$

The bottom half-equation, with its more positive $E^{\ominus}$ value, gains electrons and will proceed in a forward direction. The top half-equation, with its less positive $E^{\ominus}$ value, supplies electrons and will proceed in a backward direction. Therefore $Fe^{3+}$ is reduced to $Fe^{2+}$ and nickel atoms are oxidised to

$Ni^{2+}$ ions. The overall chemical equation for the reaction that takes place in the cell is:

$$Ni + 2Fe^{3+} \rightarrow Ni^{2+} + 2Fe^{2+}$$

This means that in the nickel half-cell nickel metal is oxidised to $Ni^{2+}$ ions. In the iron half-cell $Fe^{3+}$ ions are reduced to $Fe^{2+}$ ions. The cell voltage is 1.02 V, with the iron half-cell as the positive pole. The electrons supplied by the $Ni^{2+}/Ni$ half-cell flow to the $Fe^{3+}/Fe^{2+}$ half-cell through the external circuit. They don't flow through the salt bridge. This is shown in *figure 2.17*.

In order to write the equation:

$$Ni + 2Fe^{3+} \rightarrow Ni^{2+} + 2Fe^{2+}$$

the $Fe^{3+}/Fe^{2+}$ half-equation was doubled so that both half-equations would involve two electrons. This does not mean that the $E^{\ominus}$ value of +0.77 V had to be doubled when working out the cell voltage. Cell voltages are always correctly calculated using the $E^{\ominus}$ values as listed. In this case, +0.77 V − (−0.25 V) = +1.02 V.

## SAQ 2.13

Look at the section 'Using $E^{\ominus}$ values to predict cell voltages' on page 12. Give the equation for the overall chemical reaction that takes place in the following cells:

a   the $Ag/Ag^+$, $Zn/Zn^{2+}$ cell
b   the $Fe^{2+}/Fe^{3+}$, $Cu/Cu^{2+}$ cell
c   the cell in SAQ 2.9
d   the cell in SAQ 2.10.
e   Draw each electrochemical cell and show the direction of flow of electrons in the external circuit, as in *figure 2.17*.

# Limitations of the standard electrode potential approach

As we have seen, standard electrode potentials are measured under standard conditions:

■ a temperature of 298 K
■ a pressure of one atmosphere
■ all concentrations at 1.00 mol dm⁻³.

The actual conditions for a reaction either in a lab or in industry are unlikely to be standard. Under

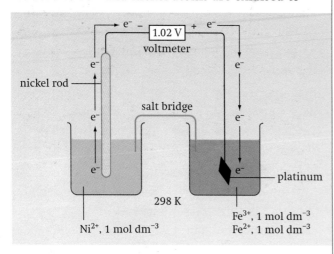

● **Figure 2.17** Electrons flow from the $Ni/Ni^{2+}$ half-cell to the $Fe^{3+}/Fe^{2+}$ half-cell.

such conditions the $E^{\ominus}$ values for the relevant half-equations are still a useful guide to what will or will not occur. If the $E^{\ominus}$ values of the two half-equations involved differ by more than 0.30 V then the reaction predicted by the $E^{\ominus}$ values will nearly always be the one that occurs, even under non-standard conditions of temperature, pressure or concentration.

Where the $E^{\ominus}$ values of the two half-equations are closer than 0.30 V, the actual conditions must be taken into account.

If a half-cell is constructed with non-standard concentrations, its electrode potential can be measured using a standard hydrogen electrode as the other half-cell. The voltage measured is now an $E$ value, not an $E^{\ominus}$ value. Increasing the concentration of a substance on the left of the half-equation will make the $E$ value more positive (or less negative) than $E^{\ominus}$. Increasing the concentration of a substance on the right of the half-equation will make the $E$ value less positive (or more negative) than $E^{\ominus}$. For example, under standard conditions

$$Fe^{3+} + e^- \rightleftharpoons Fe^{2+}; \qquad\qquad E^{\ominus} = +0.77\,V$$

- If $[Fe^{3+}]$ is more than $1.00\,mol\,dm^{-3}$, $E$ might be $+0.85\,V$ (i.e. greater than $E^{\ominus}$).
- If $[Fe^{3+}]$ is less than $1.00\,mol\,dm^{-3}$, $E$ might be $+0.70\,V$.
- If $[Fe^{2+}]$ is more than $1.00\,mol\,dm^{-3}$, $E$ might be $+0.70\,V$.
- If $[Fe^{2+}]$ is less than $1.00\,mol\,dm^{-3}$, $E$ might be $+0.85\,V$.

---

0.30 V is given here as a *rough guide* figure only. If $E^{\ominus}$ values differ by over 0.30 V then the reaction predicted by the $E^{\ominus}$ value is *nearly always* the one that occurs. If $E^{\ominus}$ values differ by less than 0.30 V, non-standard conditions *may well* result in an unexpected outcome. If this leaves you desiring a bit more precision, you will have to find out about the Nernst equation!

---

SAQ 2.14

The half-cell

$$Cr_2O_7{}^{2-} + 14H^+ + 6e^- \rightleftharpoons 2Cr^{3+} + 7H_2O$$

has an $E^{\ominus}$ value of $+1.33\,V$. All concentrations in the solutions used to measure this value are, of course, $1.00\,mol\,dm^{-3}$.

a Suggest an $E$ value if:
   (i) $[Cr_2O_7{}^{2-}]$ were to be increased
   (ii) $[H^+]$ were to be decreased
   (iii) $[Cr^{3+}]$ were to be increased.
b What effect would each of these concentration changes have on the strength of the $Cr_2O_7{}^{2-}$ solution as an oxidising agent?
c What conditions would you use to make a solution of $Cr_2O_7{}^{2-}$ as strong an oxidising agent as possible?
d Use Le Chatelier's principle to explain your answer to part c.

---

A well-known example of the effect of non-standard conditions is the reaction of $MnO_2$ with concentrated HCl to make chlorine. This reaction involves $MnO_2$ being reduced to $Mn^{2+}$ under acid conditions while $Cl^-$ ions are oxidised to $Cl_2$. The relevant half-equations are:

$$MnO_2 + 4H^+ + 2e^- \rightleftharpoons Mn^{2+} + 2H_2O; \qquad E^{\ominus} = +1.23\,V$$
$$\tfrac{1}{2}Cl_2 + e^- \rightleftharpoons Cl^-; \qquad\qquad\qquad\quad E^{\ominus} = +1.36\,V$$

The $E^{\ominus}$ values predict that $MnO_2$ *cannot* oxidise $Cl^-$ ions to $Cl_2$ under standard conditions (in fact, chlorine should be able to oxidise $Mn^{2+}$ to $MnO_2$). However, the $E^{\ominus}$ values are close enough for non-standard concentrations to make a difference. If concentrated HCl is used, the concentrations of $H^+$ and $Cl^-$ will be well over $1.00\,mol\,dm^{-3}$. Under these conditions the $E$ values might be:

$$\tfrac{1}{2}Cl_2 + e^- \rightleftharpoons Cl^-; \qquad\qquad\qquad\quad E = +1.30\,V$$
$$MnO_2 + 4H^+ + 2e^- \rightleftharpoons Mn^{2+} + 2H_2O; \qquad E = +1.40\,V$$

This predicts that under such conditions $MnO_2$ will oxidise $Cl^-$ ions to chlorine, which is what is observed.

$$Ni + 2e^- + 2Fe^{2+} \rightarrow Ni^{2+} + 2Fe^{3+} + 2e^-$$

# Reaction rate has a role to play too

The rate of a particular reaction may also lead to a prediction based on $E^\ominus$ values proving unsatisfactory. Standard electrode potentials can tell you whether or not a particular redox reaction will take place but *not* whether or not it takes place at a useful rate. If predicted to happen, the reaction may happen at an unacceptably slow rate. The $E^\ominus$ values can tell us nothing about the rate of the reaction.

One example of this is the lack of a reaction between zinc metal and water. Water contains $H^+$ ions. The relevant half-equations are :

$$Zn^{2+} + 2e^- \rightleftharpoons Zn; \qquad\qquad E^\ominus = -0.76\,V$$
$$H^+ + e^- \rightleftharpoons \tfrac{1}{2}H_2; \qquad\qquad E^\ominus = 0.00\,V$$

The concentration of $H^+$ ions in water is well below $1.00\,mol\,dm^{-3}$, but even when this is taken into account, these $E^\ominus$ values predict that the reaction

$$Zn + 2H^+ \rightarrow Zn^{2+} + H_2$$

should occur. Any reaction that does take place, however, is too slow to be observed. Although $E^\ominus$ values predict that zinc should react with water at $298\,K$ to give $Zn^{2+}$ ions and hydrogen gas, $E^\ominus$ values cannot predict whether or not this reaction occurs at a reasonable rate. It doesn't! The reaction between zinc and water is very slow indeed.

## SAQ 2.15

Summarise briefly the two limitations to using $E^\ominus$ values to predict the feasibility of a reaction.

## SAQ 2.16

If an industrial process relied on a reaction that was impractically slow under normal conditions how might the chemical engineers in charge try to solve the problem? You should use your knowledge of reaction rates to suggest several different approaches.

# SUMMARY

- A half-cell can contain either an element electrode in contact with its aqueous ions, or two different aqueous ions of the same element in two different oxidation states using platinum as the electrode.

- The standard electrode potential of a half-cell, $E^\ominus$ is defined as the voltage of the half-cell compared with a standard hydrogen electrode.

- The standard electrode potential of a half-cell is a measure in volts of the ease with which one oxidation state in the half-cell can be converted into the other oxidation state.

- Standard conditions are necessary when measuring an $E^\ominus$ value.

- Two half-cells put together form an electrochemical cell. The cell voltage of an electrochemical cell can be calculated by finding the difference between the standard electrode potentials of the two half-cells.

- A particular redox reaction will occur if the standard electrode potential of the half-equation involving the species being reduced is more positive than the standard electrode potential of the half-equation involving the species being oxidised.

- Balanced equations can be written for the reaction taking place in an electrochemical cell.

- Under non-standard concentrations a different reaction from the one predicted by standard electrode potentials may take place.

- Although a reaction predicted by standard electrode potentials will occur spontaneously it may be very slow.

# Questions

1  The $E^\ominus$ value for the $Mn^{3+}/Mn^{2+}$ half-cell is +1.49 V.

a  Write a half-equation for the $Mn^{3+}/Mn^{2+}$ half-cell.

b  Draw a fully labelled diagram of the electrochemical cell you would set up to measure the $E^\ominus$ value of the $Mn^{3+}/Mn^{2+}$ half-cell. Include all essential conditions.

c  Write a chemical equation for the reaction that takes place in this electrochemical cell.

2  This question is about the 2+ and 3+ aqueous ions of manganese, iron and cobalt. The relevant $E^\ominus$ values are:

$Mn^{3+} + e^- \rightleftharpoons Mn^{2+}$;          $E^\ominus = +1.49$ V
$Fe^{3+} + e^- \rightleftharpoons Fe^{2+}$;           $E^\ominus = +0.77$ V
$Co^{3+} + e^- \rightleftharpoons Co^{2+}$;          $E^\ominus = -0.28$ V

a  Which is the strongest oxidising agent out of $Mn^{3+}$, $Fe^{3+}$ and $Co^{3+}$? Which is the weakest?

b  Which is the strongest reducing agent out of $Mn^{2+}$, $Fe^{2+}$ and $Co^{2+}$? Which is the weakest?

c  Which ion can oxidise $Fe^{2+}$ to $Fe^{3+}$?

d  Which ion can reduce $Fe^{3+}$ to $Fe^{2+}$?

e  If $Mn^{3+}/Mn^{2+}$, $Fe^{3+}/Fe^{2+}$ and $Co^{3+}/Co^{2+}$ half-cells were made, which two of these together would give an electrochemical cell with the largest cell voltage? What would that voltage be? What would be the positive pole of the cell? Write an equation for the cell reaction that would take place.

3  Look at the electrochemical cell illustrated in figure 2.18.

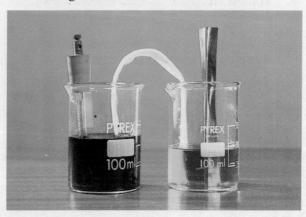

● Figure 2.18

The two half-cells are:

$MnO_4^- + 8H^+ + 5e^- \rightleftharpoons Mn^{2+} + 4H_2O$;
                                  $E^\ominus = +1.52$ V

$Cu^{2+} + 2e^- \rightleftharpoons Cu$;           $E^\ominus = +0.34$ V

a  What is the cell voltage?

b  Which half-cell is the positive pole of the cell?

c  Does this mean:
(i)  $Cu^{2+}$ ions can oxidise $Mn^{2+}$ ions to $MnO_4^-$ ions *or*
(ii) $MnO_4^-$ ions in acid solution can oxidise $Cu$ atoms to $Cu^{2+}$ ions?

d  Write a balanced equation for the overall chemical reaction that takes place in the cell.

**4** Since $Mn^{3+}$ may be reduced to $Mn^{2+}$ and $Mn^{2+}$ may be oxidised to $Mn^{3+}$, the half-equation can be written as a reversible reaction:

$$Mn^{3+} + e^- \rightleftharpoons Mn^{2+}; \qquad E^\ominus = +1.49\,V$$

Changing the concentration of either ion shifts the position of equilibrium. This means the tendency for the reaction to go forwards or backwards is changed. This causes the $E$ value to change.

**a** Suggest an $E$ value for a $Mn^{3+}/Mn^{2+}$ half-cell if $[Mn^{3+}]$ is $2.00\,mol\,dm^{-3}$ and $[Mn^{2+}]$ is $0.500\,mol\,dm^{-3}$.

**b** Suggest an $E$ value for a $Mn^{3+}/Mn^{2+}$ half-cell if $[Mn^{3+}]$ is $0.500\,mol\,dm^{-3}$ and $[Mn^{2+}]$ is $2.00\,mol\,dm^{-3}$.

**c** Use Le Chatelier's principle to explain your answers.

## Using cell voltage to predict whether or not a reaction will occur – alternative approach

On page 13 the possibility of a reaction occurring was assessed by looking at the $E^\ominus$ values of the two half-equations involved. The half-equation with the more positive $E^\ominus$ value will proceed forwards, gaining electrons. The half-equation with the less positive $E^\ominus$ value proceeds backwards, supplying electrons. An alternative approach involves manipulation of the two half-equations, followed by examination of the sign of the cell voltage. *It is recommended that you choose only one of these two approaches in predicting whether or not a reaction occurs.*

We shall explain the cell voltage approach using worked examples.

### Example 1. Can bromine oxidise silver metal to $Ag^+$ ions?

The cell voltage approach begins with an equation for the reaction under question. For this example the equation is:

$$\tfrac{1}{2}Br_2 + Ag \rightarrow Br^- + Ag^+$$

This equation must then be broken down into two half-equations:

$$\tfrac{1}{2}Br_2 + e^- \rightleftharpoons Br^-$$
$$Ag \rightleftharpoons Ag^+ + e^-$$

The $E^\ominus$ value for each half-equation is now included. The value is always the data book value and is never a multiple of it. However, for the half-equation that has been written as an oxidation, the sign of the $E^\ominus$ must be reversed. For the bromine half-equation the value is simply the data book value of $E^\ominus$, $+1.07\,V$, as the half-equation is written in the conventional way, as a reduction. For the silver half-equation the data book value of $E^\ominus$ for the reduction

$$Ag^+ + e^- \rightleftharpoons Ag$$

is $+0.80\,V$. The sign of this $E^\ominus$ value must be reversed as the process is written as an oxidation, giving $-0.80\,V$.

$$\tfrac{1}{2}Br_2 + e^- \rightleftharpoons Br^-; \qquad +1.07\,V$$
$$Ag \rightleftharpoons Ag^+ + e^-; \qquad -0.80\,V$$

The two half-equations are now added, and so are the voltages:

$$\tfrac{1}{2}Br_2 + Ag \rightarrow Br^- + Ag^+; \qquad +0.27\,V$$

Since $+0.27\,V$ is the difference between the two $E^\ominus$ values it will be the measured cell voltage if an electrochemical cell is set up with a $Br_2/Br^-$ half-cell and a $Ag^+/Ag$ half-cell. Here the *sign* of the cell voltage is of great importance. If this process produces a *positive* cell voltage, the reaction as written will occur. This reaction therefore *does* occur, i.e. bromine and silver react to give silver bromide. Bromine will oxidise silver. If the process had produced a *negative* voltage the reaction as written would not occur.

Example 2. Can iodine oxidise silver metal to $Ag^+$ ions?

The equation is:

$$\tfrac{1}{2}I_2 + Ag \rightarrow I^- + Ag^+$$

The half-equations and voltages are:

$$\tfrac{1}{2}I_2 + e^- \rightleftharpoons I^-; \qquad\qquad +0.54\,V$$
$$Ag \rightleftharpoons Ag^+ + e^-; \qquad\qquad -0.80\,V$$

The two half-equations are now added, and so are the voltages:

$$\tfrac{1}{2}I_2 + Ag \rightarrow I^- + Ag^+; \qquad\qquad -0.26\,V$$

The sign of the cell voltage is negative. The reaction does not occur; iodine and silver do not react to give silver iodide. Iodine cannot oxidise silver.

Example 3. Can bromine oxidise copper metal to $Cu^{2+}$ ions?

The equation is:

$$Br_2 + Cu \rightarrow 2Br^- + Cu^{2+}$$

The half-equations and voltages are:

$$Br_2 + 2e^- \rightleftharpoons 2Br^-; \qquad\qquad +1.07\,V$$
$$Cu \rightleftharpoons Cu^{2+} + 2e^-; \qquad\qquad -0.34\,V$$

In order to balance the number of electrons the normal bromine half-equation has been multiplied by two but the $E^\ominus$ value has *not* been multiplied. $E^\ominus$ values are *never* multiplied in this or any other method. The normal copper half-equation has been reversed, so the sign of the $E^\ominus$ value for $Cu^{2+}/Cu$ has been reversed.

The two half-equations are now added, and so are the voltages:

$$Br_2 + Cu \rightarrow 2Br^- + Cu^{2+}; \qquad\qquad +0.73\,V$$

The sign of the cell voltage is positive. The reaction occurs; bromine and copper react to give copper (II) bromide. Bromine can oxidise copper atoms to copper ions.

## SAQ 2.12 – ALTERNATIVE VERSION

Use the cell voltage method to answer SAQ 2.12 (page 15). Remember that if one half-equation needs multiplying up in order to balance the overall equation for electrons, the $E^\ominus$ value should not be multiplied up.

# CHAPTER 3

# Ligands and complexes

## By the end of this chapter you should be able to:

1 state what is meant by *coordination number*;

2 predict the formula and charge of a *complex ion*, given the metal ion, its charge and the *ligand*;

3 know that complex ions with four ligands can be *planar* or *tetrahedral*;

4 know that complex ions with six ligands are *octahedral*;

5 describe *cis–trans isomerism* and *optical isomerism* in complex ions;

6 describe the use of *cis*-platin as an anti-cancer drug.

## Transition metal ions form complex ions

Transition element ions such as $Fe^{2+}$ ions in aqueous solution form a special association with water molecules. Six water molecules can each donate one lone-pair to an $Fe^{2+}$ ion, forming *dative* or *coordinate bonds* to it (*figure 3.1*). The $Fe^{2+}$ ion and its six bonded water molecules are called a **complex ion**. The ion is written $[Fe(H_2O)_6]^{2+}$. A complex ion consists of a central metal ion with one or more negative ions or neutral molecules coordinately bonded to it. $Fe^{2+}$ and other transition metal ions can form complex ions in solid compounds as well as in solutions.

The transition metals typically form complex ions in this way. The donor of the electron pairs – water in the case of $[Fe(H_2O)_6]^{2+}$ – is called the **ligand**. Each water molecule donates one lone-pair to the $Fe^{2+}$ ion, so water is a **monodentate** ligand. Other ligands can donate two lone-pairs **(bidentate)** (*table 3.1*). Ligands donating more than one lone-pair are generally known as **polydentate** ligands.

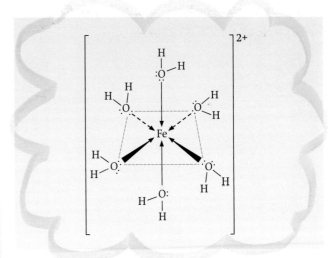

● **Figure 3.1** $[Fe(H_2O)_6]^{2+}$.

| Type of ligand | Formula | Name |
|---|---|---|
| monodentate | $H_2O$ | water |
| | $NH_3$ | ammonia |
| | CO | carbon monoxide |
| | $Cl^-$ | chloride ion |
| | $CN^-$ | cyanide ion |
| | $NO_2^-$ | nitrite ion |
| | $SCN^-$ | thiocyanate ion |
| bidentate | $NH_2CH_2CH_2NH_2$ | ethane-1,2-diamine (en) |

● **Table 3.1** Some of the more common ligands.

## SAQ 3.1

What is meant by the following terms?
a   complex ion
b   ligand
c   polydentate ligand

The **number of coordinate bonds formed between the ligands and the transition metal ion is called the coordination number** of the complex ion. Typically the coordination number of a complex ion is **four or six.**

■ Where the ligands are monodentate, this simply means four or six ligands bond to the central ion, for example $[Ni(CN)_4]^{2-}$ and $[Co(NH_3)_6]^{3+}$ (*figure 3.2*).

■ With bidentate ligands, such as ethane-1,2-diamine (abbreviated to 'en'), this means two or three ligands bond to the central ion. $[Ni(en)_3]^{2+}$ is a good example, with a coordination number of six (*figure 3.3*).

■ Examples of complex ions involving bidentate ligands and a coordination number of four are rare and need not concern us.

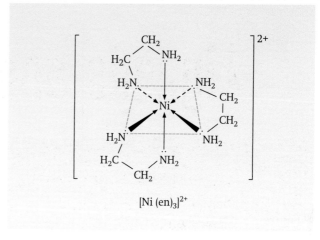

● **Figure 3.3**  $[Ni(en)_3]^{2+}$ – an example of a complex ion containing bidentate ligands.

## SAQ 3.2

a   What is meant by the term 'coordination number'?
b   What is the coordination number of the transition metal ion in the following complexes?
   (i) $[Fe(NH_3)_6]^{3+}$       (iii) $[Co(en)_3]^{3+}$
   (ii) $[CoCl_4]^{2-}$        (iv) $[AuCl_4]^{-}$
c   What is the charge on the central transition metal ion in each complex?

# The shapes of complex ions

Where the coordination number is four, the shape of the complex ion will either be **square planar or tetrahedral** (*figure 3.4*).

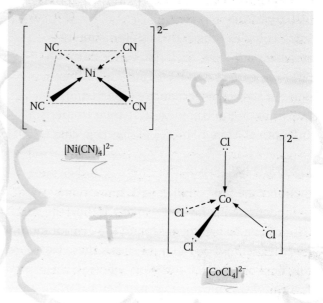

● **Figure 3.4**  $[Ni(CN)_4]^{2-}$ is square planar; $[CoCl_4]^{2-}$ is tetrahedral.

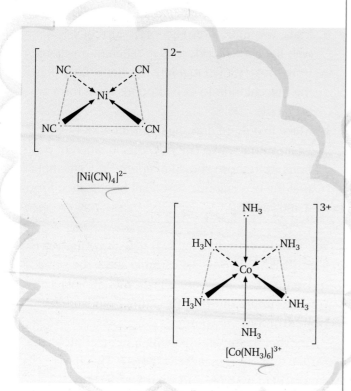

● **Figure 3.2**  $[Ni(CN)_4]^{2-}$ and $[Co(NH_3)_6]^{3+}$ – examples of complex ions containing monodentate ligands.

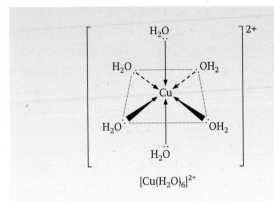

● **Figure 3.5** $[Cu(H_2O)_6]^{2+}$ is octahedral.

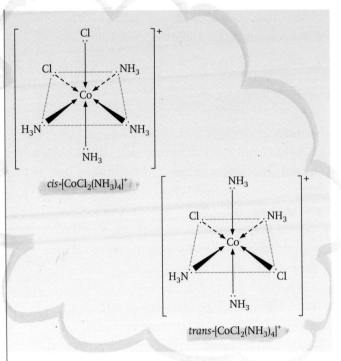

● **Figure 3.6** *Cis*-$[CoCl_2(NH_3)_4]^+$ and *trans*-$[CoCl_2(NH_3)_4]^+$.

Where the coordination number is six, the shape of the complex ion will be octahedral (*figure 3.5*). Notice how *figure 3.5* attempts to convey the three-dimensional shape and avoids depicting a planar, hexagonal shape, which would be incorrect.

## SAQ 3.3

Draw the 3D shapes of the following complex ions:
**a** $[Fe(NH_3)_6]^{3+}$
**b** $[AuCl_4]^-$ (square planar)
**c** $[FeCl_4]^{2-}$ (tetrahedral).

# Stereoisomerism in transition metal complexes

Some complex ions exist as **stereoisomers**. Stereoisomers have the same bonds but with different spatial arrangements. Two different types of **stereoisomerism** are observed in transition metal complexes: *cis–trans* isomerism and optical isomerism (see *Chemistry 2*, chapter 6).

## Cis–trans isomerism

In an octahedral complex with four of one monodentate ligand and two of another, the six ligands can be arranged around the central ion in two different ways. *Figure 3.6* shows these two ways for the $[CoCl_2(NH_3)_4]^+$ ion. Notice how in the *cis* form the two chloride-to-cobalt bonds form a 90° angle with each other, while in the *trans* form the two chloride-to-cobalt bonds form a 180° angle

with each other. In drawing these **isomers** it is again important to draw carefully so that the shape of the molecule is clear.

## SAQ 3.4

**a** Make two more drawings of *cis*-$[CoCl_2(NH_3)_4]^+$ with the two chloride ions in different positions from those shown in *figure 3.6*. Remember that the two chloride-to-cobalt bonds must form a 90° angle.
**b** Make two more drawings of *trans*-$[CoCl_2(NH_3)_4]^+$, again with the two chloride ions in different positions from those shown in *figure 3.6*. Remember that the two chloride-to-cobalt bonds must form a 180° angle.

You should note that the two new drawings of *cis*-$[CoCl_2(NH_3)_4]^+$ in SAQ 3.4a simply show the same *cis* isomer from different viewpoints. In SAQ 3.4b you are simply showing the same *trans* isomer from different viewpoints.

Another example, involving a neutral molecule rather than an ion, is $[NiCl_2(NH_3)_2]$. This has a square planar shape and therefore has two stereoisomers (*figure 3.7*). Note that *cis–trans* isomerism is not seen in tetrahedral complexes.

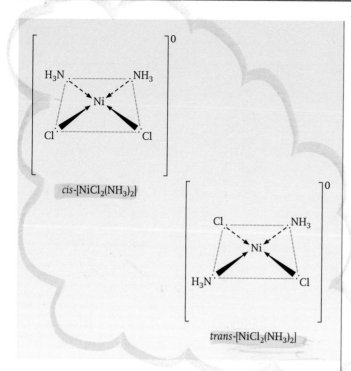

$cis\text{-}[NiCl_2(NH_3)_2]$

$trans\text{-}[NiCl_2(NH_3)_2]$

● **Figure 3.7** *Cis*-[NiCl$_2$(NH$_3$)$_2$] and *trans*-[NiCl$_2$(NH$_3$)$_2$].

## *Cis*-platin

The compound known as platin has the formula [PtCl$_2$(NH$_3$)$_2$]. It exists as two stereoisomers. The shape of the platin molecule is therefore square planar. The two stereoisomers are shown in *figure 3.8*. The difference between these two stereo-isomers is very important.

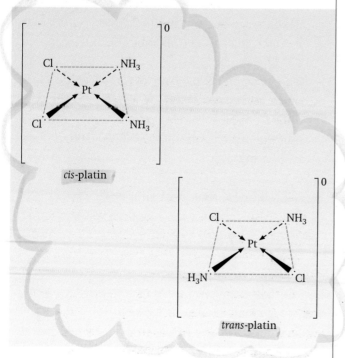

*cis*-platin

*trans*-platin

● **Figure 3.8** *Cis*-platin and *trans*-platin.

Platin binds to the DNA in fast-growing cells. When cells grow they copy their DNA and then they divide into two 'daughter' cells. Each daughter cell gets one copy of the DNA. In the presence of platin the two daughter cells have incorrectly copied DNA, due to the effect of the bound-on platin. Because of the incorrectly copied DNA the cells die.

*Cis*-platin binds much more effectively than *trans*-platin to DNA in the fast-growing cells in cancers. *Cis*-platin is therefore used as an anti-cancer drug; this form of treatment is called chemotherapy. *Cis*-platin has been particularly successful in treating testicular cancer, causing survival rates to increase from 5% to 80% by 1999.

## Optical isomerism

Some octahedral complexes can exist in two forms that are non-superimposable mirror images of each other.

In order to understand this 'non-superimpos-able mirror image' concept, consider your left and right hands. Your right hand, when viewed in a mirror, looks exactly like your left hand viewed directly, and vice versa, so they are 'mirror images' of each other. However, if you try to put your right hand in exactly the same shape as your left hand, you can't, because the fingernails and knuckles of one hand will face downwards while those of the other hand face upwards. They are 'non-superimposable'.

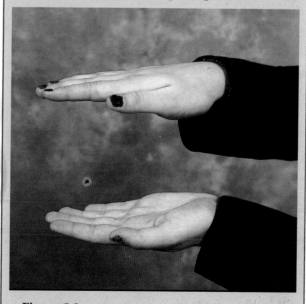

● **Figure 3.9**

An example of a compound that shows optical isomerism is $[Ni(en)_3]^{2+}$ (see *box 3A*). The two forms are shown in *figure 3.10*.

### Box 3A Optical isomerism

Normally a sample of $[Ni(en)_3]^{2+}$ contains equal amounts of the two optical isomers. If the two forms are separated from each other, then a pure sample of one form is found to rotate the plane of polarised light. This type of stereoisomerism is therefore known as **optical isomerism**. The two isomers rotate polarised light in opposite directions, one clockwise and the other anticlockwise. In the original mixture these two effects cancel each other out, so no rotation of polarised light is seen.

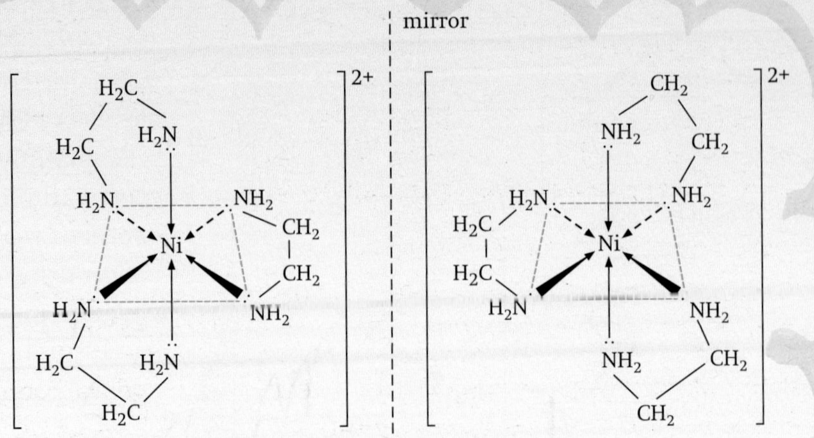

● **Figure 3.10** The two forms of $[Ni(en)_3]^{2+}$ are mirror images of each other, but they are not superimposable. They are optical isomers.

## SAQ 3.5

The compound $[CoCl_2(en)_2]$, a neutral molecule, exists in three isomeric forms (*figure 3.11*). They consist of two *cis* isomers and one *trans* isomer, the two *cis* isomers being non-superimposable mirror images of each other.

**a** Which diagram shows the *trans* isomer?

**b** What type of isomerism is shown by the two *cis* isomers?

**c** Redraw the two *cis* isomers in a way that emphasises that they are in fact non-superimposable mirror images of each other.

**d** Does $[CoCl_2(en)_2]$ contain $Co^{2+}$ or $Co^{3+}$ ions?

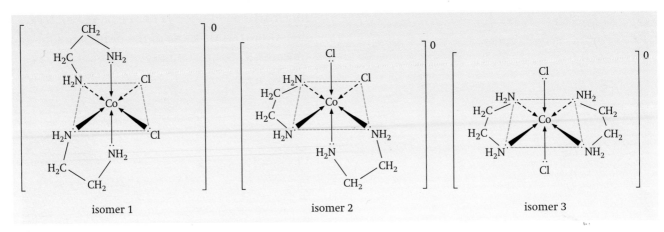

● **Figure 3.11** $[CoCl_2(en)_2]$ exists in three isomeric forms.

# SUMMARY

- A complex ion consists of a central transition metal ion surrounded by ions or molecules called ligands.

- A ligand has an atom with one or more lone-pairs. Ligands bond to transition metal ions by one or more coordinate bonds.

- A ligand that bonds to the transition metal ion by one coordinate bond using one lone-pair is said to be monodentate.

- A ligand that bonds to the transition metal ion by two coordinate bonds using two lone-pairs is said to be bidentate.

- If the ligands make a total of four coordinate bonds to the transition metal ion, that ion is said to have a coordination number of four.

- The shape of a four-coordinate complex may be square planar or tetrahedral.

- If the ligands make a total of six coordinate bonds to the transition metal ion, that ion is said to have a coordination number of six.

- The shape of a six-coordinate complex will be octahedral.

- Octahedral or square planar complexes involving a suitable combination of ligands can show stereoisomerism involving *cis* and *trans* isomers.

- The compound platin has *cis* and *trans* isomers. *Cis*-platin is a powerful drug used in cancer treatment.

- Octahedral complexes involving suitable bidentate ligands or a suitable combination of ligands can show stereoisomerism involving optical isomers.

# Questions

1  Using the ligands $Cl^-$, $NH_3$ and $NH_2CH_2CH_2NH_2$, draw and clearly label diagrams of octahedral complexes of chromium(III) that show the following types of isomerism:

a  *cis–trans*

b  optical.

Indicate clearly the overall charge on each complex ion you draw.

(UCLES)

2  Chromium forms compounds with the formula $CrCl_3.6H_2O$, containing various octahedral chromium(III) complexes. One such compound is violet and another pale green. When an excess of aqueous silver nitrate was added separately to solutions containing 0.01 mole of each compound, the mass of silver chloride precipitated in each case was found to be 4.31 g from the violet complex, but only 2.87 g from the green complex.

Given the fact that $Cl^-$ ions that are part of the chromium(III) complex will not be free to combine with silver ions and form silver chloride, deduce the formulae of the chromium-containing ions in the two compounds.

(UCLES)

3  Nickel(II) bromide and cobalt(II) bromide each form a complex with the mono-dentate organic ligand triethylphosphine ($R_3P$, where R is $C_2H_5$: note that $R_3P$ behaves like ammonia as a ligand).

The complexes have the following general formula:

$M(R_3P)_2Br_2$ where M = Ni or Co

The nickel complex occurs in two isomeric forms, one of which has an overall dipole while the other does not. The cobalt complex, however, occurs in only one form.

a  In terms of the different stereo-chemistries of the complexes formed, suggest explanations for these observations.

b  Predict, with a reason, whether or not the cobalt complex has an overall dipole.

(UCLES)

# CHAPTER 4

# Colour

**By the end of this chapter you should be able to:**

1 describe the shape and symmetry of the five 3d orbitals;

2 describe the *splitting* of d-orbital energy levels in octahedral transition metal complexes;

3 explain, in terms of d-orbital splitting, the absorption of some frequencies of visible light by transition metal complexes;

4 explain why ions with partially filled d orbitals form *coloured complexes*;

5 explain why ions with either zero or ten electrons in their d orbitals form colourless solutions or white solids;

6 explain changes in colour of complexes due to the change in d-orbital splitting resulting from *ligand substitution*;

7 suggest the colour of a transition metal complex from its visible spectrum;

8 describe the use of d-block elements in pigments and the paint industry, for example $TiO_2$ in white paint and Monastral pigments in coloured paints.

## Why are things coloured?

Some things, such as yellow–orange sodium lamps (*figure 4.1*) and the red star Betelgeuse (*figure 4.2*), are coloured because they are making light themselves and the light they make is coloured. Most coloured objects, however, are coloured because when ordinary 'white' light falls on them they absorb some of the colours in the light.

● **Figure 4.2** The red star Betelgeuse (top left), part of the constellation Orion the Hunter.

● **Figure 4.1** The distinctive yellow/orange light from sodium lamps.

Visible white light is a mixture of many colours: when these colours are separated out by a triangular glass prism or a shower of raindrops we call the colours a spectrum or rainbow (*figure 4.3*). You are reading this page in visible light. The paper reflects *all* the visible light to your eyes, so it looks white. The ink reflects *none* of the visible light, so it looks black.

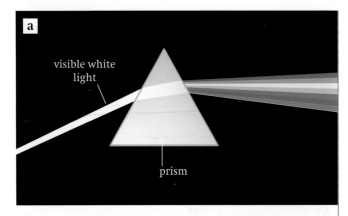

● **Figure 4.3** The splitting of white light: **a** by a prism and **b** by water droplets.

The photograph of manganese(III) chloride solution in *figure 4.4* looks red because the dyes on the paper are absorbing all the colours in visible light *except* red. Only the red is reflected to your eyes, so that is how you see it. If you put a beaker of manganese(III) chloride solution on the table in front of you now it will look red; it is absorbing all other colours and the red you see will have been transmitted by the solution. *Box 4A* summarises how colours appear in solutions and solids.

● **Figure 4.4**
Manganese(III)
chloride solution.

**Box 4A**
**Where does colour come from?**

■ Transparent solutions that transmit all wavelengths of visible light appear colourless (*figure 4.5a*).
■ Opaque objects that reflect all wavelengths of visible light appear white (*figure 4.5b*).
■ Coloured solutions absorb some wavelengths of visible light and transmit other wavelengths – the colour we see comes from the transmitted light (*figure 4.5c*).
■ Coloured solids absorb some wavelengths of visible light and reflect other wavelengths – the colour we see comes from the reflected light (*figure 4.5d*).

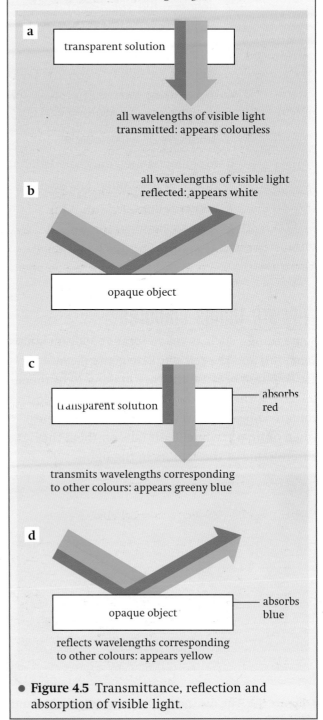

● **Figure 4.5** Transmittance, reflection and absorption of visible light.

This absorption of colour is going to be central to the explanation of why some transition metal complexes are coloured, and why some are not. The absorption is caused by electrons in d orbitals. To begin with, a description of the shape of the d orbitals is necessary.

## SAQ 4.1

**a** Why does copper(II) sulphate appear blue?
**b** Why does chromium(III) chloride appear green?
**c** Why does potassium chromate(VI) appear yellow?

## The orbitals in the 3d subshell

The 3d subshell can accommodate ten electrons. Since only two electrons can go into any one orbital, this means there are five orbitals in the 3d subshell. The five orbitals are shown in *figure 4.6*. These five orbitals all have the same energy – they are said to be degenerate.

In an ion that only has a single electron in the 3d subshell, such as an isolated $Ti^{3+}$ ion, this electron can move freely between the five orbitals without absorbing or releasing energy. Isolated transition metal atoms or ions with between one

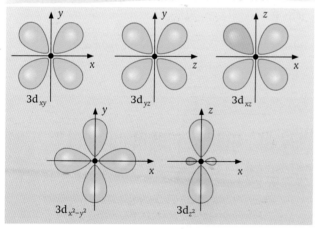

● **Figure 4.6** The 3d electron subshells.

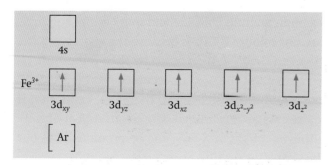

● **Figure 4.7** $Fe^{3+}$ has the electronic configuration $[Ar] 3d^5 4s^0$.

and nine electrons in the 3d subshell can have these electrons in any of these orbitals, except for the fact that electrons won't pair unless they have to. For example, $Fe^{3+}$ has the electronic configuration shown in *figure 4.7*.

## SAQ 4.2

Use the 'electrons in boxes' notation to show the electronic configuration of the following isolated species:
**a** $Fe^{2+}$       **c** $Cu^{2+}$
**b** Fe atom       **d** Cr atom.

The five 3d orbitals are only degenerate (have the same energy) if the atom or ion involved is isolated. This is not the case for the five 3d orbitals in a transition metal complex – they are not isolated and so they are *not* degenerate. In an octahedral complex the six lone-pairs from the ligands form six coordinate bonds along the same axes as the $3d_{z^2}$ and $3d_{x^2-y^2}$ orbitals. This causes the $3d_{z^2}$ and $3d_{x^2-y^2}$ orbitals to become of higher energy than the $3d_{xy}$, $3d_{xz}$ and $3d_{yz}$ orbitals (*figure 4.8*). This is called **d-orbital splitting**. The five 3d orbitals in an octahedral transition metal complex are *not* degenerate – they no longer all have the same energy. The energy gap is labelled $\Delta E$. 'd-orbital splitting' means that the five orbitals in the 3d subshell are split into a sub-group of higher energy and a sub-group of lower energy. This is shown in *figure 4.8*. It does *not* mean that individual 3d orbitals split apart.

## SAQ 4.3

**a** Explain the meaning of the following terms:
  (i) d-orbital splitting
  (ii) $\Delta E$.
**b** What is the cause of d-orbital splitting?

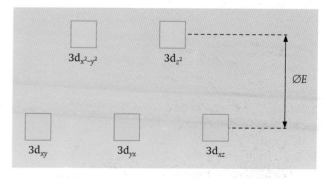

● **Figure 4.8** d-orbital splitting in an octahedral complex.

## Electron promotion

If a transition metal complex has at least one electron in a lower 3d orbital and at least one gap in an upper 3d orbital, an electron can move from the lower 3d orbital to the upper 3d orbital. The electron is said to be **promoted**. As this happens, some of the visible light shining on the complex is absorbed. The light supplies the energy for the promotion. Only one colour of light will be absorbed, however, and that will be the colour with exactly the correct energy (see box 4B). The colours that are not absorbed are transmitted, so we see them. Because some of the colours have been absorbed, the light transmitted to us is no longer white. It is coloured, so that is how the complex looks to us. An example of this is shown in figure 4.9.

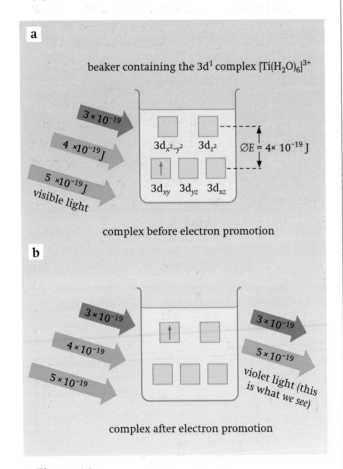

● Figure 4.9

a Visible light 'hits' the 3d$^1$ complex. The d-orbital splitting in this complex corresponds to an energy of 4 × 10$^{-19}$ J.

b The complex absorbs the green light, as its energy is 4 × 10$^{-19}$ J. The complex transmits the red and blue light. The red and blue light mix to give violet. The complex looks violet to us.

## SAQ 4.4

a What is meant by the 'promotion' of an electron?

b Why is only one colour of visible light absorbed to supply energy for this process?

c What happens to the visible light that is not absorbed?

---

### Box 4B Quantum theory

Light is a form of energy; it supplies energy in tiny packets called *quanta*. The size of one packet (a 'quantum') of light energy depends on the frequency of the light – the number of light waves per second, measured in hertz. The size of a quantum of energy is found by multiplying the frequency of the light by Planck's constant, which is 6.63 × 10$^{-34}$ J s. The symbol for Planck's constant is $h$, so, if frequency is $f$ and energy quantum size is $e$:

$$e = hf$$

For visible light of frequency 6 × 10$^{14}$ Hz:

$$e = 6.63 \times 10^{-34} \text{ J s} \times 6 \times 10^{14} \text{ s}^{-1}$$
$$= 3.98 \times 10^{-19} \text{ J}$$

This may be a tiny amount of energy, but it could be exactly enough to promote an electron from a lower 3d orbital to a higher one. If it is, the electron will absorb the quantum of light energy as it is promoted. Electron promotion cannot use light quanta that are too big, leaving a bit left over. Neither can it use light quanta that are too small, waiting for a bit more to come along. The quanta absorbed must be exactly the right size.

## Why are many compounds not coloured?

All atoms and ions contain electrons and have vacant higher energy orbitals that the outer electrons *could* be promoted to. This promotion will absorb energy. However, many substances, for example sodium chloride and magnesium sulphate, are not coloured. This is because the energy gap between the orbital occupied by their outermost electrons and the next unoccupied orbital is too large to absorb visible light. Therefore, 'light' that is more energetic is needed. The electrons *may* absorb ultraviolet light or X-rays, and be promoted, but our eyes can't detect this. Such substances reflect every colour of the visible light that hits them, so they appear white.

There are three key factors in making transition metal complexes coloured:
  (i)   the size of the energy gap caused by d-orbital splitting
  (ii)  at least one of the d orbitals must be occupied by an electron
  (iii) at least one of the d orbitals must not be fully occupied.

Some compounds of d-block metals are colourless.
■ In the case of titanium(IV) oxide, the $Ti^{4+}$ ions have the electronic configuration [Ar] $3d^0$ $4s^0$. Point (ii) above is not satisfied – there are no 3d electrons to be promoted.
■ *All* scandium compounds are [Ar] $3d^0$, so they are all colourless/white, unless the anion is coloured.
■ In the case of copper(I) chloride, the $Cu^+$ ions are [Ar] $3d^{10}$ $4s^0$. Point (iii) above is not satisfied – there are no vacant higher 3d orbitals to promote electrons into.
■ *All* zinc compounds are $3d^{10}$, so they are all colourless/white, unless the anion is coloured.

● **Figure 4.10** The pigment in this white paint is titanium(IV) oxide. It is white because the $Ti^{4+}$ ions have no occupied d orbitals – they reflect all the visible light that hits them. Titanium(IV) oxide pigments are the purest white pigments available and they have excellent hiding power, so they are good at obliterating any colour being painted over.

*SAQ 4.5*

**a** Which of the following compounds would you expect to be coloured?
  (i)    CuI
  (ii)   $NiSO_4$
  (iii)  $TiCl_3$
  (iv)   $TiCl_4$
  (v)    $ZnSO_4$
  (vi)   $MnCl_2$
  (vii)  $FeSO_4$
  (viii) $ZnCrO_4$

**b** Give a reason for each compound you expect to be colourless.

## Transition elements in paints

Transition metal complexes are often used in paints. As well as the use of the titanium(IV) oxide pigment in white paints (*figure 4.10*), they are used to make many coloured pigments. In fact, for brilliance and clarity of colour, transition metal complexes with organic ligands cannot be bettered. Examples of such pigments include Monastral blue, in which $Cu^{2+}$ ions are complexed by phthalocyanine ligands (*figure 4.11*). If hydrogen atoms in the phthalocyanine ligand are replaced by chlorine or bromine atoms, the colour of the pigment can be changed to other blue shades or to various shades of green.

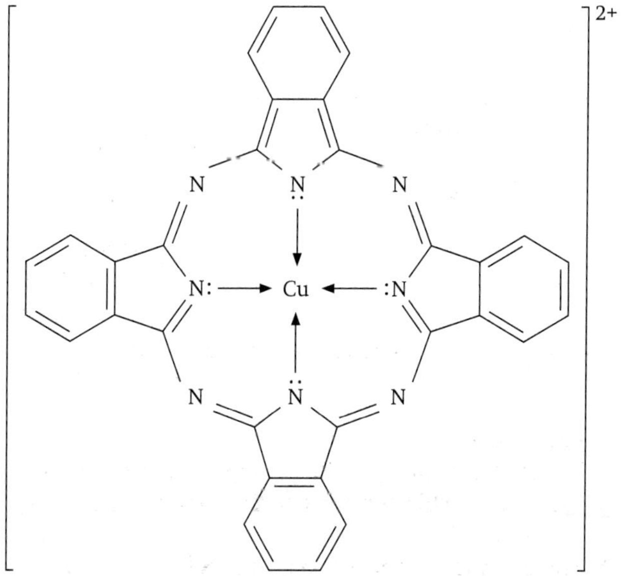

● **Figure 4.11** This $Cu^{2+}$–phthalocyanine complex is the blue pigment called Monastral blue.

[CuCl₄]²⁻

This yellow complex forms on adding concentrated HCl.

Start here

[Cu(H₂O)₆]²⁺

The well-known blue Cu²⁺ complex with water.

[Cu(H₂O)₂(NH₃)₄]²⁺

This dark blue complex forms on adding concentrated NH₃.

● **Figure 4.12** The equations for the changes are:
$$[Cu(H_2O)_6]^{2+} + 4Cl^- \rightleftharpoons [CuCl_4]^{2-} + 6H_2O$$
$$[Cu(H_2O)_6]^{2+} + 4NH_3 \rightleftharpoons [Cu(H_2O)_2(NH_3)_4]^{2+} + 4H_2O$$

# Ligand substitution

As you will remember from *Chemistry 2*, chapter 11, if a different ligand is added to a solution of a complex ion, **ligand substitution** takes place. This is also called **ligand exchange** or **ligand displacement**. With different ligands the size of the energy gap, $\Delta E$, changes. If $\Delta E$ gets larger, then light of a higher energy is absorbed; if $\Delta E$ gets smaller, then light of a lower energy is absorbed. Either way the colour of the complex will change. *Figure 4.12* shows two changes that can occur to the well-known blue $[Cu(H_2O)_6]^{2+}$ complex.

## SAQ 4.6

Write a balanced chemical equation for each of the following observations. Include formulae for all the complex ions involved.

a If a solution of NaCN is added to an aqueous solution of an $Fe^{3+}$ salt, the six water ligands around the $Fe^{3+}$ ion are replaced by six $CN^-$ ions, forming a new complex ion.

b If a solution of NaCN is added to an aqueous solution of an $Fe^{2+}$ salt, the six water ligands around the $Fe^{2+}$ ion are replaced by six $CN^-$ ions, forming a new complex ion.

c If ethylenediamine (en) is added to an aqueous solution of a $Ni^{2+}$ salt, the six water ligands around the $Ni^{2+}$ ion are replaced by three en molecules.

## SAQ 4.7

Why do modifications to the phthalocyanine ligand in a Monastral pigment change the colour of the pigment?

There are two possible explanations if the colour of a transition metal complex changes on adding another reagent.
■ Firstly, ligand substitution, as discussed here.
■ Secondly, the transition metal ion in the complex may have been oxidised or reduced to a different oxidation state (see chapter 1, page 2).
In order to decide which is the correct explanation, ask yourself:
■ Will something in the reagent added be able to act as a ligand?
■ Is something in the reagent added an oxidising agent or a reducing agent?

Look at the magenta transition metal complex in *figure 4.13*. It is magenta (a reddy-blue colour) because it absorbs green light; we see the red and blue. Reaction 1 shows a different ligand being added to it. This produces a complex ion with a *bigger* $\Delta E$. The new complex absorbs more energetic light, blue, so we see the red and green. The new complex looks yellow, since yellow is what our eyes see when red *and* green light arrive together from the same object. Reaction 2 shows another different ligand being added to it. This produces a complex ion with a *smaller* $\Delta E$. The new complex absorbs less energetic light, red, so we see the blue and green. The new complex looks cyan (a greeny-blue colour).

Remember the following.

Larger $\Delta E$:

- light absorbed is of higher energy
- light absorbed has smaller wavelength and higher frequency
- light absorbed is towards blue end of spectrum
- complex appears yellow or red.

Smaller $\Delta E$:

- light absorbed is of lower energy
- light absorbed has longer wavelength and lower frequency
- light absorbed is towards red end of spectrum
- complex appears cyan or blue.

# The spectra of transition metal complexes

If visible light is shone through a coloured complex, the coloured light that comes out can be analysed by a **visible spectrometer**. This separates out the emergent light into a spectrum, and measures its wavelength and intensity. The spectrum is called a visible spectrum because visible light is being used. A typical visible spectrum is shown in *figure 4.14*. Notice that the vertical axis is labelled 'relative absorption'. The horizontal axis is labelled with the wavelength of light in nanometres (1 nm = $1 \times 10^{-9}$ m) and the corresponding colours are shown below. The absorption at the right shows that the $Cu(H_2O)_6{}^{2+}$ complex is absorbing at the red and yellow end of the spectrum. Green and blue light are not being absorbed, so we see $Cu(H_2O)_6{}^{2+}$ as a greeny-blue colour.

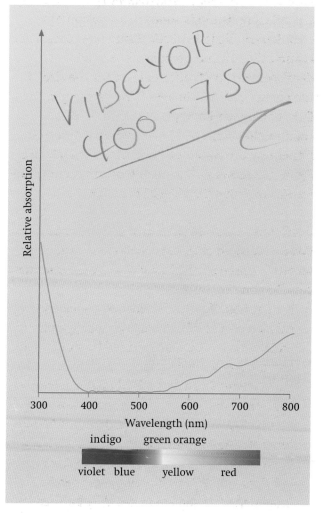

● **Figure 4.14** A simplified absorption spectrum of $Cu(H_2O)_6{}^{2+}$.

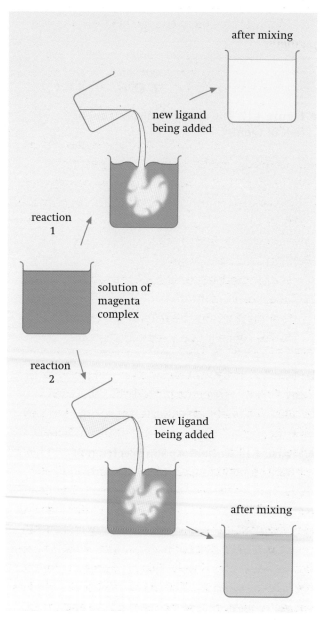

● **Figure 4.13** Colour changes due to changes in ligand.

## SAQ 4.8

Use the visible spectra in *figures 4.15–4.18* to predict the colour of the following transition metal complex ions:

**a** $[Ti(H_2O)_6]^{3+}$

**b** $[Cr(NH_3)_6]^{3+}$

**c** *cis*-$[CoCl_2(en)_2]^+$

**d** *trans*-$[CoCl_2(en)_2]^+$

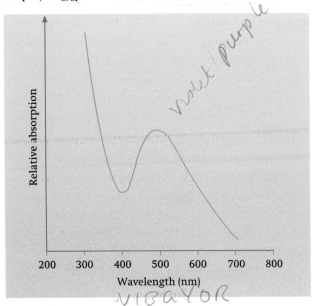

● **Figure 4.15** The absorption spectrum of $[Ti(H_2O)_6]^{3+}$.

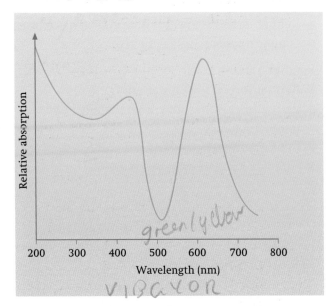

● **Figure 4.17** The absorption spectrum of *cis*-$[CoCl_2(en)_2]^+$.

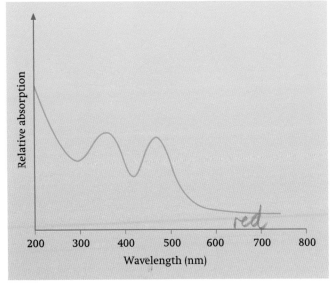

● **Figure 4.16** The absorption spectrum of $[Cr(NH_3)_6]^{3+}$.

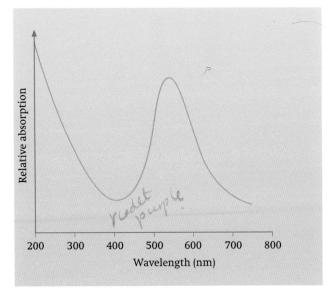

● **Figure 4.18** The absorption spectrum of *trans*-$[CoCl_2(en)_2]^+$.

# SUMMARY

- In octahedral complexes two of the 3d orbitals of the central transition metal ion have a higher energy than the other three 3d orbitals. This is called d-orbital splitting.

- The size of the energy gap between the lower and upper 3d orbitals is called $\Delta E$.

- In a complex with split 3d orbitals, electrons can be promoted from a lower 3d orbital to an upper 3d orbital, absorbing one colour of visible light as they do so. This makes the complex appear coloured.

- In transition metal ions that are $3d^0$ or $3d^{10}$, electrons cannot be promoted from a lower 3d orbital to an upper 3d orbital, so no visible light is absorbed. Compounds and complexes containing such ions appear colourless.

- A particular transition metal ion will show differing amounts of splitting with different ligands. Ligand substitution therefore changes the colour of the ion, since $\Delta E$ changes.

- Titanium(IV) oxide is white because $Ti^{4+}$ is $3d^0$. It is used extensively as a pigment in white paint.

- Certain organic ligands produce transition metal complexes with brilliant colours. These are used as pigments in the paint industry, e.g. Monastral blue.

- A visible spectrum of a coloured species tells us what colours of visible light are absorbed by the species and enables us to predict its colour.

# Questions

**1** **a** Explain why aqueous ions containing transition metals are coloured, whereas aqueous ions of other metals are usually colourless. (You may wish to use $[Cr(H_2O)_6]^{3+}$ and $[Al(H_2O)_6]^{3+}$ as examples.)

**b** The visible spectra of solutions of two $Cr^{3+}$ complexes, A and B, are shown in *figure 4.19.*

  (i) What are the colours of solutions A and B?

  (ii) The spectra show that the peak in the curve for solution B is at a longer wavelength than is the peak in the curve for solution A. What deduction can be made from this fact about the size of the d-orbital splitting in the two complexes?

**2** Identify the species involved in the following series of reactions and explain the sequence.

The addition of aqueous ammonia to a yellow solution of copper(II) chloride in dilute hydrochloric acid causes the colour to change successively to green, pale blue, and finally a dark blue solution, after the intermediate formation of a pale blue precipitate.

*(UCLES)*

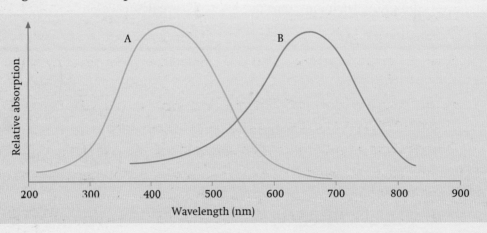

● **Figure 4.19**

# CHAPTER 5

# Case studies of four metals

## By the end of this chapter you should be able to:

1 know the formulae and colours of aqueous ions and compounds containing vanadium in the +2, +3, +4 and +5 oxidation states;

2 use $E^{\ominus}$ data to predict the redox chemistry of vanadium in the +2, +3, +4 and +5 oxidation states;

3 explain how $V_2O_5$ acts as a catalyst in the Contact process;

4 know the formulae, relative stability and colours of aqueous ions and compounds containing chromium in the +3 and +6 oxidation states;

5 describe and explain the interconversion of chromate(VI) and dichromate(VI);

6 recall the use of chromium in steel alloys;

7 know the formulae, relative stability and colours of aqueous ions and compounds containing cobalt in the +2 and +3 oxidation states;

8 know how variations of ligand and temperature affect the stability and geometry of certain cobalt complexes;

9 know the formulae, relative stability and colours of aqueous ions and compounds containing copper in the +1 and +2 oxidation states;

10 understand why $Cu^+$ disproportionates in aqueous solutions;

11 understand the reaction between $Cu^{2+}$ and $I^-$ and how it is used quantitatively in the estimation of copper in alloys such as brass;

12 recall the use of copper as a constituent of brass, bronze, coinage metals and other alloys.

## Vanadium

Element 23, vanadium, is hard, steely grey and very resistant to corrosion. It forms a wide range of stable compounds in the +2, +3, +4 and +5 oxidation states. Examples of these are shown in *figure 5.1*.

### SAQ 5.1

a Use the rules in chapter 1 (page 3) to confirm that the oxidation states shown in *figure 5.1* are 0, +2, +3, +4 and +5.

b *Figure 5.1* shows the characteristic colours of vanadium in the +2, +3, +4 and +5 oxidation states. Learn them, then test yourself on them after half an hour and again after two hours.

You should notice that in the lower oxidation states vanadium is found as simple ions, i.e. $V^{2+}$ and $V^{3+}$. In the higher oxidation states, +4 and +5, vanadium is found in ions containing oxygen, i.e. $VO^{2+}$, $VO_2^+$ and $VO_3^-$. This is common amongst transition metals.

*yesterdays beautiful garden* [handwritten]

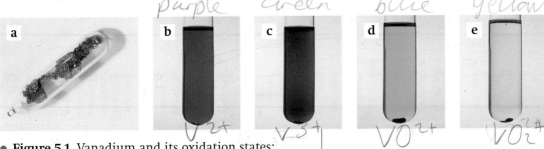

purple    green    blue    yellow [handwritten labels]

V²⁺    V³⁺    VO²⁺    VO₂²⁺ [handwritten labels]

● **Figure 5.1** Vanadium and its oxidation states:
**a** vanadium metal;
**b** a solution containing $V^{2+}$ ions;
**c** a solution containing $V^{3+}$ ions;
**d** a solution containing $VO^{2+}$ ions;
**e** a solution containing $VO_2^+$ ions.

A lower oxidation state of vanadium can be converted to a higher oxidation state by an oxidising agent. A higher oxidation state of vanadium can be converted to a lower oxidation state by a reducing agent. A good example of such a reducing agent is zinc metal. It will reduce $VO_2^+$ to $VO^{2+}$, then to $V^{3+}$, and finally to $V^{2+}$. Zinc will carry out these reductions one step at a time, so all the colours in *figure 5.1* can be seen one after the other.

## SAQ 5.2

Write a balanced equation for each of the following reductions. Use $E^{\ominus}$ values from page 50 to explain why each reaction occurs.
**a** Zinc can reduce $VO_2^+$ to $VO^{2+}$ in acid solution.
**b** Zinc can reduce $VO^{2+}$ to $V^{3+}$ in acid solution.
**c** Zinc can reduce $V^{3+}$ to $V^{2+}$.

## SAQ 5.3

Zinc cannot reduce $V^{2+}$ to V metal. Explain why this is so using $E^{\ominus}$ values from page 50.

## SAQ 5.4

If a large excess of $Fe^{3+}(aq)$ is added to an acidic solution of $V^{2+}$, will the $V^{2+}$ be oxidised? If so, to what final state? Justify your answers using $E^{\ominus}$ values from page 50.

## SAQ 5.5

If a large excess of $SO_2(aq)$ is added to an acidic solution of $VO_2^+$, will the $VO_2^+$ be reduced? If so, to what final state? Justify your answers with cell voltages.

## $V_2O_5$ as a catalyst in the contact process

It is said that sulphuric acid is *the* most important industrial chemical. If this is true, then $V_2O_5$ must be the most important catalyst, as it catalyses the reaction

$$SO_2 + \tfrac{1}{2}O_2 \rightarrow SO_3$$

Sulphur dioxide is easy to make by burning sulphur in air. Once you've made sulphur trioxide it combines very easily with water to make sulphuric acid. Unfortunately the

$$SO_2 + \tfrac{1}{2}O_2 \rightarrow SO_3$$

step is slow because it has a very large activation energy. In the presence of $V^{5+}$ and $O^{2-}$ ions it goes in two stages:

$$SO_2 + \tfrac{1}{2}O_2 + 2V^{5+} + O^{2-} \rightarrow SO_3 + \tfrac{1}{2}O_2 + 2V^{4+}$$
$$SO_3 + \tfrac{1}{2}O_2 + 2V^{4+} \rightarrow SO_3 + O^{2-} + 2V^{5+}$$

Each of these stages has a low activation energy, and so proceeds quickly. $V_2O_5$ acts as a catalyst by providing an alternative pathway of lower activation energy (*figure 5.2*). It can do this because

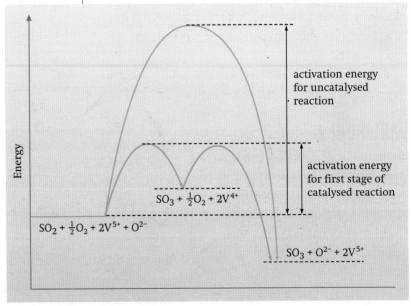

activation energy for uncatalysed reaction

activation energy for first stage of catalysed reaction

$SO_3 + \tfrac{1}{2}O_2 + 2V^{4+}$

$SO_2 + \tfrac{1}{2}O_2 + 2V^{5+} + O^{2-}$

$SO_3 + O^{2-} + 2V^{5+}$

Energy

● **Figure 5.2** The course of reaction involving $V_2O_5$ as a catalyst.

vanadium forms stable compounds in more than one oxidation state. $V_2O_5$ enables sulphuric acid to be made more quickly, because it speeds up the reaction

$$SO_2 + \tfrac{1}{2}O_2 \rightarrow SO_3$$

This reaction is the slowest step in the production of sulphuric acid. The $V_2O_5$ is not used up as it speeds up the reaction, so it is acting as a catalyst.

## SAQ 5.6

a  Write equations for:
  (i)  the formation of sulphur dioxide
  (ii)  the combination of sulphur trioxide with water.
b  Look again at the two-stage process for making sulphur trioxide in the presence of a $V_2O_5$ catalyst. Identify the species oxidised and the species reduced in each stage.
c  Vanadium shows here a typical transition metal property, which results in $V_2O_5$ being a good catalyst. What is the property?
d  Why does the presence of $V_2O_5$ speed up the formation of sulphur trioxide?

# Chromium

Element 24, chromium, is hard but brittle, and has an attractive silvery appearance which has led to it coating the bumpers and other bits of bicycles and cars.

Chromium forms compounds in the +2, +3, +4, +5 and +6 oxidation states, out of which +3 and +6 are the two most often seen in chromium compounds.

An oxyanion is a positively charged ion containing oxygen. In the +6 state chromium forms two

● **Figure 5.3** The ultimate in chrome headlights.

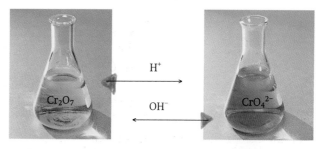

● **Figure 5.4** The interconversion of $K_2CrO_4$(aq) and $K_2Cr_2O_7$(aq).

different oxyanions. These are the orange dichromate(VI) ion, $Cr_2O_7^{2-}$, and the yellow chromate(VI) ion, $CrO_4^{2-}$. They are commonly used as potassium salts, potassium dichromate(VI), $K_2Cr_2O_7$, and potassium chromate(VI), $K_2CrO_4$. In solution each of these oxyanions can be converted into the other by altering the pH, since the following equilibrium exists:

$$Cr_2O_7^{2-} + H_2O \rightleftharpoons 2CrO_4^{2-} + 2H^+$$

$Cr_2O_7^{2-}$ is formed in acidic solution, while $CrO_4^{2-}$ is the ion formed in alkaline solution (*figure 5.4*).

## SAQ 5.7

Explain why $Cr_2O_7^{2-}$ is formed in acidic solution and $CrO_4^{2-}$ is formed in alkaline solution. You should refer to Le Chatelier's principle and the equation

$$Cr_2O_7^{2-} + H_2O \rightleftharpoons 2CrO_4^{2-} + 2H^+$$

in your answer.

---

The interconversion of $Cr_2O_7^{2-}$ and $CrO_4^{2-}$ can be shown as an equilibrium in three different ways:

$$Cr_2O_7^{2-} + H_2O \rightleftharpoons 2CrO_4^{2-} + 2H^+$$
$$Cr_2O_7^{2-} + OH^- \rightleftharpoons 2CrO_4^{2-} + H^+$$
$$Cr_2O_7^{2-} + 2OH^- \rightleftharpoons 2CrO_4^{2-} + H_2O$$

All three versions are valid and predict the same outcome – $CrO_4^{2-}$ is formed in alkaline solution, $Cr_2O_7^{2-}$ is formed in acidic solution.

---

Potassium dichromate(VI) in acid solution is a strong oxidising agent, being reduced to $Cr^{3+}$ ions, which are very stable:

$$Cr_2O_7^{2-} + 14H^+ + 6e^- \rightleftharpoons 2Cr^{3+} + 7H_2O; \ E^{\ominus} = +1.33\,V$$

*#020760180099*

● **Figure 5.5** A violet solution of $[Cr(H_2O)_6]^{3+}$.

In aqueous solution $Cr^{3+}$ forms the violet $[Cr(H_2O)_6]^{3+}$ complex ion. However, when potassium dichromate(VI) in acid solution is used as an oxidising agent, the colour change observed is from orange to green. This is illustrated in *figure 5.6*. Particularly when hot, $[Cr(H_2O)_6]^{3+}$ undergoes ligand substitution reactions forming green species. This is the reason why most solutions and solids containing $Cr^{3+}$ are green.

## SAQ 5.8

a What is the coordination number of chromium in $[Cr(H_2O)_6]^{3+}$?
b What will be the shape of the $[Cr(H_2O)_6]^{3+}$ complex ion? Illustrate your answer with a diagram.
c Explain what is meant by ligand substitution and why ligand substitution changes the colour of $[Cr(H_2O)_6]^{3+}$ solutions.
d Sketch *possible* visible spectra of violet and green solutions containing $Cr^{3+}$.

● **Figure 5.6**
a This mixture contains potassium dichromate(VI), sulphuric acid and ethanol.
b After boiling under reflux for half an hour, the mixture contains $Cr^{3+}$, sulphuric acid and ethanoic acid.

## SAQ 5.9

Look at *figure 5.6a*.
a Which substance is being oxidised?
b Which substance is being reduced?
c Why is sulphuric acid necessary?
d The half-equation for the oxidation of ethanol is:

$$C_2H_5OH + H_2O \rightleftharpoons CH_3COOH + 4H^+ + 4e^-$$

Write a balanced chemical equation for the reaction in *figure 5.6a*.

# Uses of chromium

In 1913, Harry Brearley, a Sheffield chemist, was trying to find new steel alloys for making gun barrels. One particular alloy, containing about 13% chromium, proved useless for this purpose, so he threw his test piece outside on to his ever-growing scrap heap. Some months later he noticed that while all the other bits of scrap had rusted, this piece hadn't.

After further investigation and scientific fiddling around, Brearley settled on an alloy consisting of 70% iron, 20% chromium and 10% nickel as the ideal 'stainless steel'. The chromium and nickel in the alloy quickly form a layer composed of their oxides on the surface of the steel when it first comes in contact with the air. Unlike iron oxide, which is flaky and porous, this oxide layer is tenacious and impervious to air and water – it protects the steel underneath.

If smaller amounts of chromium are added to steel, the resulting alloy is very hard. Steel hardened in this way is used for making many tools.

● **Figure 5.7** Because the stainless steel doesn't rust, the De Lorean didn't need painting.

# Cobalt

Element 27, cobalt, is a hard, unreactive, white metal with a slightly blue appearance. It forms a wide range of compounds in the +2 and +3 oxidation states, of which the +2 state is usually the most stable. $Co^{2+}$ forms the stable $[Co(H_2O)_6]^{2+}$ ion, which is pink – as are most octahedral $Co^{2+}$ complexes. Tetrahedral complexes of $Co^{2+}$, such as $[CoCl_4]^{2-}$, are mostly blue.

Cobalt chloride paper is used as a test for water. When dry, the paper is blue. Following the addition of water, the $[Co(H_2O)_6]^{2+}$ ion is formed and the paper turns pink (*figure 5.8*)

$Co^{3+}$ forms the aqueous complex $[Co(H_2O)_6]^{3+}$, which is blue. However, it is so easily reduced to $[Co(H_2O)_6]^{2+}$ that there is no simple aqueous chemistry involving the $[Co(H_2O)_6]^{3+}$ ion. There are, in fact, very few simple compounds containing $Co^{3+}$, and those that do exist, such as $CoF_3$, instantly react with water to give a $Co^{2+}$ compound. The water is oxidised in the reaction, producing oxygen gas. In complexes with ligands other than water, $Co^{3+}$ is stable, however, and this leads to the 'wide range' of compounds already referred to, exhibiting an equally wide range of colours.

## SAQ 5.10

Draw diagrams to show the shapes of the complex ions $[Co(H_2O)_6]^{2+}$ and $[CoCl_4]^{2-}$.

$[Co(H_2O)_6]^{2+}$ is a good example of a complex ion that changes colour due to ligand substitution. The change

$$\overset{pink}{[Co(H_2O)_6]^{2+}} + 4Cl^- \rightarrow \overset{blue}{[CoCl_4]^{2-}} + 6H_2O$$

takes place in $CoCl_2(aq)$ if either a high concentration of $Cl^-$ or a high temperature is applied.

## SAQ 5.11

**a** What colour change is observed when concentrated HCl is added to a solution containing $[Co(H_2O)_6]^{2+}$? Explain why this change takes place by reference to Le Chatelier's principle.

**b** Explain why it is reasonable to expect that the reaction

$$[Co(H_2O)_6]^{2+} + 4Cl^- \rightarrow [CoCl_4]^{2-} + 6H_2O$$

is endothermic.

An example of the enhanced stability of $Co^{3+}$ with different ligands is the stability of $[Co(NH_3)_6]^{3+}$. Compare the $E^\circ$ values:

$$\overset{blue}{[Co(H_2O)_6]^{3+}} + e^- \rightleftharpoons \overset{pink}{[Co(H_2O)_6]^{2+}}; \qquad E^\circ = +1.81\,V$$

$$\overset{brown}{[Co(NH_3)_6]^{3+}} + e^- \rightleftharpoons \overset{dark\ brown}{[Co(NH_3)_6]^{2+}}; \qquad E^\circ = +0.11\,V$$

A wide variety of reducing agents can reduce $[Co(H_2O)_6]^{3+}$ to $[Co(H_2O)_6]^{2+}$, including water, iodide ions and silver metal. The reduction of $[Co(NH_3)_6]^{3+}$ to $[Co(NH_3)_6]^{2+}$ requires much stronger reducing agents, however, like iron metal or $V^{2+}$ ions. The enhanced stability of $[Co(NH_3)_6]^{3+}$ is due to ammonia being a stronger ligand than water i.e. ammonia forms stronger dative bonds.

## SAQ 5.12

Write balanced ionic equations for the following.

**a** The reduction of $[Co(H_2O)_6]^{3+}$ by $I^-$ ions (which are oxidised to $I_2$).

**b** The reduction of $[Co(H_2O)_6]^{3+}$ by Ag atoms (which are oxidised to $Ag^+$).

**c** The reduction of $[Co(NH_3)_6]^{3+}$ ions by Fe atoms (which are oxidised to $Fe^{2+}$).

**d** The reduction of $[Co(NH_3)_6]^{3+}$ ions by $V^{2+}$ ions (which are oxidised to $V^{3+}$).

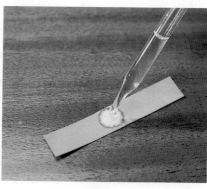

● **Figure 5.8** Anhydrous cobalt chloride paper is blue. Is the drop of liquid water? The pink-coloured complex $[Co(H_2O)_6]^{2+}$ proves it is.

● **Figure 5.9** A bronze incense burner stand, made in Cyprus, 1200 BC. The person is shown carrying a copper ingot.

# Copper

Element 29, copper, is a reddish-gold colour. It is soft and ductile, and its ability to conduct heat and electricity is second only to silver. It was first smelted from its ores over 5500 years ago. Early metallurgists in Cyprus produced very pure copper, so the metal was named after the island.

Copper forms a wide range of stable compounds in the +2 oxidation state but, unlike most other transition metals, copper also forms compounds in the +1 oxidation state. While compounds and complexes containing $Cu^{2+}$ are virtually all green or blue, compounds containing $Cu^+$ are white solids.

## SAQ 5.13

a  What is the electronic structure of:
  (i) a copper atom
  (ii) a $Cu^{2+}$ ion
  (iii) a $Cu^+$ ion?
b  Explain why $Cu^{2+}$ compounds are coloured while $Cu^+$ compounds are not.

Aqueous solutions containing $Cu^{2+}$ ions are stable; however, aqueous solutions containing $Cu^+$ ions are not. This can be explained by looking at the $E^\ominus$ values for the reduction of $Cu^{2+}$ ions to $Cu^+$ ions and for the reduction of $Cu^+$ ions to copper atoms:

$$Cu^{2+} + e^- \rightleftharpoons Cu^+; \qquad E^\ominus = +0.15\,\text{V}$$
$$Cu^+ + e^- \rightleftharpoons Cu; \qquad E^\ominus = +0.52\,\text{V}$$

Since it has the more positive $E^\ominus$ value, the bottom reaction will proceed in a forward direction while the top reaction proceeds backwards. One $Cu^+$ ion is reduced to a copper atom *by a second $Cu^+$ ion*. This second $Cu^+$ ion is oxidised to a $Cu^{2+}$ ion *by the first $Cu^+$ ion*. This simultaneous oxidation and reduction of the same species is called **disproportionation**. $Cu^+$ ions are not stable in aqueous solution because they disproportionate to give Cu atoms and $Cu^{2+}$ ions.

$$2Cu^+ \longrightarrow Cu^{2+} + Cu$$

## SAQ 5.14

a  Draw a diagram of an electrochemical cell consisting of a $Cu^{2+}/Cu^+$ half-cell and a $Cu^+/Cu$ half-cell.
b  What will be the cell voltage?
c  Which half-cell is the positive pole of the cell?
d  Write an equation for the overall cell reaction.

## SAQ 5.15

a  Copper(I) sulphate disproportionates immediately when added to water. Write an equation for this reaction and describe what you would expect to *see* during the reaction.
b  Why is it difficult to set up the electrochemical cell you have drawn in answer to SAQ 5.14, part **a**?

● **Figure 5.10** Copper(II) sulphate.

CuSO4 - blue

● **Figure 5.11** Copper(II) chloride.

Cu2CL - green

● **Figure 5.12** Copper(I) iodide.

The disproportionation of $Cu^+$ ions only takes place in aqueous solution. Dry copper(I) compounds and those that are insoluble in water are therefore stable.

All the copper(I) halides are extremely insoluble in water. If a solution containing $Cu^{2+}$ ions is mixed with a solution containing an excess of iodide ions, the iodide ions will reduce the $Cu^{2+}$ ions to $Cu^+$ ions. The iodide ions are oxidised to iodine.

$$Cu^{2+} + I^- \rightarrow Cu^+ + \tfrac{1}{2}I_2$$

The $Cu^+$ ions then combine with more iodide ions to form a precipitate of copper(I) iodide:

$$Cu^+ + I^- \rightarrow CuI$$

The overall equation is therefore:

$$Cu^{2+}(aq) + 2I^-(aq) \rightarrow CuI(s) + \tfrac{1}{2}I_2(aq)$$

Although the CuI precipitate that forms is actually white, it always appears a brown colour due to the iodine that forms at the same time. The $Cu^+$ ions in CuI are stable and do not disproportionate because they are not in aqueous solution.

## SAQ 5.16

The following $E^\ominus$ values

$Cu^{2+} + e^- \rightleftharpoons Cu^+$;     $E^\ominus = +0.15\,V$
$\tfrac{1}{2}I_2 + e^- \rightleftharpoons I^-$;     $E^\ominus = +0.54\,V$

do *not* predict that $Cu^{2+}$ ions are reduced by $I^-$ ions. Suggest an explanation as to why this reaction does in fact occur. You should consider the effect the insolubility of CuI has on the concentration of $Cu^+(aq)$.

● **Figure 5.13** The copper(II) sulphate solution and potassium iodide solution have been mixed in the conical flask. A precipitate of white copper(I) iodide has formed, but it is coloured brown by iodine.

## Copper alloys

Copper is a constituent of many useful alloys.

■ Copper and zinc make brass. Its resistance to corrosion, pleasant ringing tones and attractive gold-coloured appearance all explain why brass is used to make musical instruments. Brass is harder than copper. Both metals are used in central heating systems. Being more ductile, copper is drawn out to make the pipes. Being harder, brass is more suitable for the joints, which are made by casting or machining.

■ Copper and tin make bronze. Bronze is harder than copper and is used to make statues and medals.

■ Bronze (in this case 97% copper, 2.5% zinc and 0.5% tin) is used for 1p and 2p coins. However, since September 1992, the price of copper has made it too expensive to make 1p and 2p coins out of bronze, so steel coated in a thin layer of copper has been used instead – except for some of the 2p coins issued in 1998. You can distinguish the copper-plated steel coins from the older ones with a magnet.

● **Figure 5.14** Steve Redgrave (now Sir) and Andy Holmes with their Olympic bronze medals for the coxed pairs event in Seoul, 1988.

● **Figure 5.15** The outer part of the £2 coin is 76% copper, 4% nickel and 20% zinc. The inner part is 75% copper and 25% nickel.

■ Cupro-nickel is one of the alloys used for UK coinage; it is soft enough for the coins to be made by stamping but hard enough to resist wear. The more 'silvery' looking the coin, the higher the percentage of nickel in the alloy. For example, 5p, 10p and 50p coins are 75% copper and 25% nickel, while 20p coins are 84% copper and 16% nickel.

## Analysing the amount of copper in an alloy

If a piece of brass is dissolved in nitric acid (*figure 5.16a*), the solution obtained is a mixture of copper(II) nitrate and zinc nitrate (*figure 5.16b*). Analysing this mixture can tell us how much copper it contains. If the mass of the original piece of brass is also known, then the composition of the original alloy can be calculated.

The analysis is done by adding an excess of KI(aq) to the mixture containing $Cu^{2+}$ (*figure 5.16c*). As has already been seen, this causes the precipitation of all the copper as copper(I) iodide:

$$2Cu^{2+} + 4I^- \rightarrow 2CuI + I_2$$

The amount of iodine produced can then be found by titrating the resulting mixture with a sodium thiosulphate ($Na_2S_2O_3$) solution of known concentration. The thiosulphate ions reduce the iodine back to iodide ions:

$$2S_2O_3^{2-} + I_2 \rightarrow S_4O_6^{2-} + 2I^-$$

As the end-point of this titration is neared, the brown colour due to the iodine becomes faint (*figure 5.16d*). Adding a little starch solution produces a dark blue colour (*figure 5.16e*), which in turn disappears when enough sodium

**a** The brass about to be placed in the nitric acid.

**b** The solution containing a mixture of $Zn^{2+}$ and $Cu^{2+}$ ions.

**c** The precipitate formed by adding KI, containing $Cu^+$ ions and iodine.

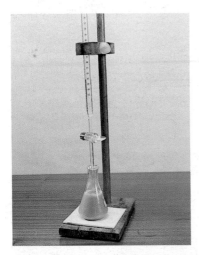

**d** Near the end-point of the titration against $Na_2S_2O_3$.

**e** Near the end-point, following the addition of starch.

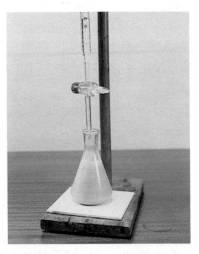

**f** At the end-point – the dark blue colour has disappeared.

● **Figure 5.16** The sequence of events in the estimating of brass.

thiosulphate solution has been added to react with all the iodine (*figure 5.16f*). The disappearance of a dark blue colour is much easier to judge accurately than the disappearance of a pale brown colour.

The two equations above show us that two $Cu^{2+}$ ions produce one iodine molecule, which then reacts in the titration with two thiosulphate ions. The number of moles of thiosulphate added in the titration is therefore the same as the number of moles of copper originally present. From this the original mass of copper in the alloy can be calculated. This measurement is known as 'estimating the composition of the alloy'. The word 'estimating' in this context does *not* suggest inaccuracy! The photos in *figure 5.16* show the sequence of events in this process.

## SAQ 5.17

A 1.00 g piece of brass is dissolved in nitric acid to produce a mixture of copper(II) nitrate and zinc nitrate solutions. An excess of potassium iodide solution is added, causing copper(I) iodide and iodine to form. The iodine formed reacts with 47.8 cm$^3$ of 0.200 mol dm$^{-3}$ sodium thiosulphate solution.

a How many moles of sodium thiosulphate were needed to react with all the iodine?

b How many moles of $Cu^{2+}$ were present before the excess of potassium iodide solution was added?

c What mass of copper is this? ($A_r$ of copper is 63.5)

d What was the percentage by mass of copper in the original piece of brass?

# SUMMARY

◆ The common aqueous ions of vanadium are $V^{2+}$ (violet), $V^{3+}$ (green), $VO^{2+}$ (blue) and $VO_2^+$ (yellow). These ions can be formed from each other by adding suitable oxidising and reducing agents.

◆ When vanadium(V) oxide acts as a catalyst in the Contact process for the manufacture of sulphuric acid, its catalytic activity depends on the oxidation number of vanadium changing from +5 to +4 and back to +5.

◆ Complexes of $Cr^{3+}$ are either green or violet. They are stable but may be oxidised to the +6 state by strong oxidising agents.

◆ In the +6 state, chromium forms chromate(VI) and dichromate(VI) ions which can be interconverted by adding $H^+$ or $OH^-$ ions. Dichromate(VI) ions are strong oxidising agents in acid solution – they are reduced to $Cr^{3+}$.

◆ Chromium is added to steel to make alloys such as stainless steel and tool steels.

◆ The blue aqueous complex $[Co(H_2O)_6]^{3+}$ is unstable as it is very easily reduced to $[Co(H_2O)_6]^{2+}$, which is pink.

◆ $Co^{3+}$ is much more stable with ammonia as ligand, forming the $[Co(NH_3)_6]^{3+}$ ion.

◆ If a solution of octahedral $[Co(H_2O)_6]^{2+}$ ions is heated in the presence of $Cl^-$ ions, or if a concentrated solution of $Cl^-$ ions is added, tetrahedral $[CoCl_4]^{2-}$ ions are formed.

◆ Copper forms $Cu^{2+}$ and $Cu^+$ ions. $Cu^{2+}$ ions are blue and stable. $Cu^+$ ions are colourless and are only stable in the absence of water. In aqueous solution $Cu^+$ ions disproportionate to Cu atoms and $Cu^{2+}$ ions. This is predicted by $E^\ominus$ values.

◆ When a solution containing $Cu^{2+}$ ions is treated with an excess of a solution containing $I^-$ ions, iodine is produced. The amount of iodine produced can be found accurately by titration with a sodium thiosulphate solution of known concentration, using starch as indicator. The results can be used to calculate the amount of copper originally present.

◆ Copper is a constituent of alloys such as bronze, brass and cupro-nickel.

# Questions

**1 a** On adding copper(I) sulphate to water, it immediately undergoes a disproportionation reaction.
   (i) Suggest, with a reason, the colour of copper(I) sulphate.
   (ii) Use data from page 50 to explain why the disproportionation reaction occurs, and write an equation for it.

**b** One method of determining the percentage of copper in a copper-containing ore is to dissolve the copper salts in an excess of sulphuric acid, add an excess of potassium iodide, and titrate the iodine formed with sodium thiosulphate solution.
   (i) Describe what you would observe when the potassium iodide is added to the acidic solution of copper salts. Write an ionic equation for the reaction.
   (ii) When a 2.0 g sample of an ore was treated in this way, 15.8 cm$^3$ of 0.100 mol dm$^{-3}$ thiosulphate was needed to react with the iodine produced. Calculate the number of moles, and hence the percentage by mass, of copper in the ore.

*(OCR)*

**2 a** 0.01 mol of a blue solution of a vanadium salt is oxidised exactly by an acidified solution containing 0.002 mol of $KMnO_4$, which is reduced to $Mn^{2+}$.
   (i) What is the oxidation state of vanadium in the blue solution?
   (ii) Use the data on page 50 to deduce the final oxidation state of the vanadium after the reaction. Write a balanced chemical equation for the reaction.
   (iii) Suggest a colour for the solution produced.

**b** Another 0.01 mol of the blue solution of a vanadium salt is reduced exactly by 0.005 mol of $Sn^{2+}$(aq). The $Sn^{2+}$ ions are oxidised to $Sn^{4+}$ ions.
   (i) Use the data on page 50 to deduce the final oxidation state of the vanadium after the reaction. Write a balanced chemical equation for the reaction.
   (ii) Suggest a colour for the solution produced.

*(OCR)*

**3** The $E^\ominus$ value for the redox system
$$[CoL_6]^{3+} + e^- \rightarrow [CoL_6]^{2+}$$
is +1.81 V for L = $H_2O$ but +0.11 V for L = $NH_3$ (where L = a ligand).
   **a** Which is the stronger ligand, ammonia or water?
   **b** Which ligand stabilises $Co^{3+}$ the most?
   **c** In which complex is $Co^{3+}$ the stronger oxidising agent?
   **d** Use the data on page 50 to explain why dilute acidic solutions of cobalt(II) salts are stable in air, but undergo oxidation after the addition of an excess of aqueous ammonia.

*(UCLES)*

4   Sodium dichromate(VI) is usually manufactured from chromium(III) sulphate by first adding aqueous alkali and then aqueous hydrogen peroxide. The resulting alkaline solution of sodium chromate(VI) is acidified and evaporated, so that sodium dichromate(VI) separates as crystals.

a   What is the colour of chromium(III) sulphate?

b   Use the following $E^\ominus$ data to calculate the $E^\ominus_{cell}$ and construct a balanced equation for the redox reaction described above.

$$CrO_4^{2-} + 4H_2O + 3e^- \rightleftharpoons Cr^{3+} + 8OH^-;$$
$$E^\ominus = -0.13\,V$$

$$H_2O_2 + 2e^- \rightleftharpoons 2OH^-; \qquad E^\ominus = +0.87\,V$$

c   What colour is the alkaline solution of sodium chromate(VI)?

d   Write an equation for the reaction that occurs when this alkaline solution is acidified.

e   What is the colour of the crystals of sodium dichromate(VI)?

*(UCLES)*

# APPENDIX

# $E^{\ominus}$ data

| Electrode reaction | $E^{\ominus}$ (V) |
|---|---|
| $Ag^+ + e^- \rightleftharpoons Ag$ | +0.80 |
| $Br_2 + 2e^- \rightleftharpoons 2Br^-$ | +1.07 |
| $Cl_2 + 2e^- \rightleftharpoons 2Cl^-$ | +1.36 |
| $Cr^{2+} + 2e^- \rightleftharpoons Cr$ | −0.91 |
| $Cr^{3+} + 3e^- \rightleftharpoons Cr$ | −0.74 |
| $Cr_2O_7^{2-} + 14H^+ + 6e^- \rightleftharpoons 2Cr^{3+} + 7H_2O$ | +1.33 |
| $Cu^+ + e^- \rightleftharpoons Cu$ | +0.52 |
| $Cu^{2+} + 2e^- \rightleftharpoons Cu$ | +0.34 |
| $Cu^{2+} + e^- \rightleftharpoons Cu^+$ | +0.15 |
| $F_2 + 2e^- \rightleftharpoons 2F^-$ | +2.87 |
| $Fe^{2+} + 2e^- \rightleftharpoons Fe$ | −0.44 |
| $Fe^{3+} + e^- \rightleftharpoons Fe^{2+}$ | +0.77 |
| $Fe^{3+} + 3e^- \rightleftharpoons Fe$ | −0.04 |
| $2H^+ + 2e^- \rightleftharpoons H_2$ | 0.00 |
| $I_2 + 2e^- \rightleftharpoons 2I^-$ | +0.54 |
| $Mn^{2+} + 2e^- \rightleftharpoons Mn$ | −1.18 |
| $MnO_4^- + 8H^+ + 5e^- \rightleftharpoons Mn^{2+} + 4H_2O$ | +1.52 |
| $Ni^{2+} + 2e^- \rightleftharpoons Ni$ | −0.25 |
| $O_2 + 4H^+ + 4e^- \rightleftharpoons 2H_2O$ | +1.23 |
| $O_2 + 2H_2O + 4e^- \rightleftharpoons 4OH^-$ | +0.40 |
| $Pb^{2+} + 2e^- \rightleftharpoons Pb$ | −0.13 |
| $SO_4^{2-} + 4H^+ + 2e^- \rightleftharpoons SO_2 + 2H_2O$ | +0.17 |
| $Sn^{4+} + 2e^- \rightleftharpoons Sn^{2+}$ | +0.15 |
| $V^{2+} + 2e^- \rightleftharpoons V$ | −1.20 |
| $V^{3+} + e^- \rightleftharpoons V^{2+}$ | −0.26 |
| $VO^{2+} + 2H^+ + e^- \rightleftharpoons V^{3+} + H_2O$ | +0.34 |
| $VO_2^+ + 2H^+ + e^- \rightleftharpoons VO^{2+} + H_2O$ | +1.00 |
| $VO_3^- + 4H^+ + e^- \rightleftharpoons VO^{2+} + 2H_2O$ | +1.00 |
| $Zn^{2+} + 2e^- \rightleftharpoons Zn$ | −0.76 |

# Answers to self-assessment questions

## Chapter 1

**1.1**  a [Ar] $3d^{10} 4s^2$
 b [Ar] $3d^5 4s^1$
 c [Ar] $3d^6 4s^2$

**1.2**  $Sc^{3+}$ is [Ar] $3d^0 4s^0$; $Zn^{2+}$ is [Ar] $3d^{10} 4s^0$. Scandium and zinc do not form at least one ion with a partially filled 3d subshell.

**1.3**  $Ti^{2+}$ is [Ar] $3d^2 4s^0$; $Ti^{3+}$ is [Ar] $3d^1 4s^0$. Titanium does form at least one ion with a partially filled 3d subshell.

**1.4**  a $Cu^{2+}$
 b Fe
 c $Cl^-$
 d $Cu^{2+}$
 e Fe

**1.5**  a +6
 b +2
 c +3
 d +6

**1.6**  a +4
 b +6
 c 0
 d +7
 e +3
 f +2

**1.7**  Fe: $0 \to +2$; reducing agent
 H: $+1 \to 0$; oxidising agent
 Cl: $-1$ and $-1$

 Fe: $0 \to +3$; reducing agent
 H: $+1 \to 0$; oxidising agent
 Cl: $-1$ and $-1$

## Chapter 2

**2.1**  For the $Fe^{2+}/Fe$ half-cell:
 a $Fe^{2+} + 2e^- \to Fe$
 b $-0.44\,V$
 c $Fe^{2+}$: $1.00\,mol\,dm^{-3}$

For the $Cr^{2+}/Cr$ half-cell:
 a $Cr^{2+} + 2e^- \to Cr$
 b $-0.91\,V$
 c $Cr^{2+}$: $1.00\,mol\,dm^{-3}$

For the $Ag^+/Ag$ half-cell:
 a $Ag^+ + e^- \to Ag$
 b $+0.80\,V$
 c $Ag^+$: $1.00\,mol\,dm^{-3}$

In all three cells the temperature must be 298 K and in the standard hydrogen electrodes the $H^+(aq)$ concentration must be $1.00\,mol\,dm^{-3}$, the $H_2$ pressure must be 1 atmosphere and electrical contact must be made by platinum.

**2.2**  $+1.52\,V$

**2.3**  298 K, all gases at pressure of 1 atmosphere, all relevant concentrations at $1.00\,mol\,dm^{-3}$.

**2.4**  Platinum does not take part in reactions.

**2.5**

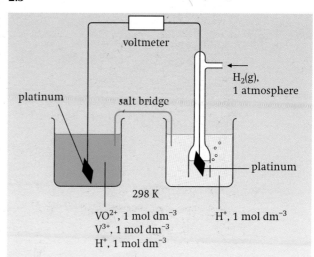

**2.6**  $S + 2e^- \rightleftharpoons S^{2-}$; $E^\oplus = -0.51\,V$

**2.7**

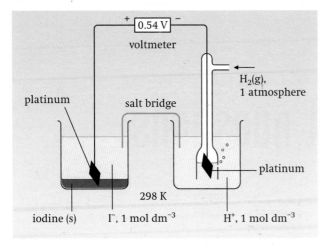

**2.8**  a  $Cr^{2+}$
     b  Ag

**2.9**  a

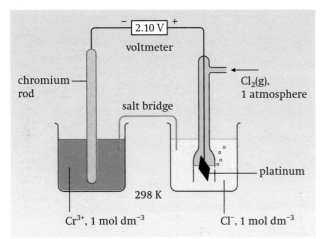

     b  2.10 V
     c  chlorine half-cell

**2.10**  a

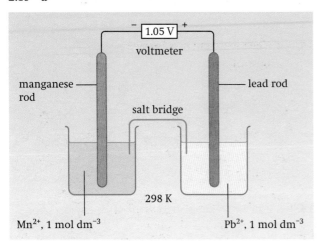

     b  1.05 V
     c  lead half-cell

**2.11**  $Fe^{3+} + I^- \rightarrow Fe^{2+} + \frac{1}{2}I_2$

**2.12**  a  yes
          $MnO_4^- + 5Cl^- + 8H^+ \rightarrow Mn^{2+} + \frac{5}{2}Cl_2 + 4H_2O$
          $MnO_4^- + 8H^+ + 5e^- \rightleftharpoons Mn^{2+} + 4H_2O$, with its *more* positive $E^\ominus$ value, will proceed in a forward direction while $Cl_2 + 2e^- \rightleftharpoons 2Cl^-$ proceeds in a backward direction.
      b  no
          $MnO_4^- + 8H^+ + 5e^- \rightleftharpoons Mn^{2+} + 4H_2O$, with its *less* positive $E^\ominus$ value, cannot proceed in a forward direction while $F_2 + 2e^- \rightleftharpoons 2F^-$ proceeds in a backward direction.
      c  yes
          $V^{2+} + H^+ \rightarrow \frac{1}{2}H_2 + V^{3+}$
          $2H^+ + 2e^- \rightleftharpoons H_2$, with its *more* positive $E^\ominus$ value, will proceed in a forward direction while $V^{3+} + e^- \rightleftharpoons V^{2+}$ proceeds in a backward direction.
      d  no
          $2H^+ + 2e^- \rightleftharpoons H_2$, with its *less* positive $E^\ominus$ value, cannot proceed in a forward direction while $Fe^{3+} + e^- \rightleftharpoons Fe^{2+}$ proceeds in a backward direction.

(**2.12** – alternative version
      a  cell voltage = +0.16 V, therefore yes
      b  cell voltage = −1.35 V, therefore no
      c  cell voltage = +0.26 V, therefore yes
      d  cell voltage = −0.77 V, therefore no)

**2.13**  a  $Zn + 2Ag^+ \rightarrow Zn^{2+} + 2Ag$
      b  $Cu + 2Fe^{3+} \rightarrow Cu^{2+} + 2Fe^{2+}$
      c  $Cr + \frac{3}{2}Cl_2 \rightarrow Cr^{3+} + 3Cl^-$
      d  $Pb^{2+} + Mn \rightarrow Mn^{2+} + Pb$
      e  On your diagrams you should have shown the following electron flow in each external circuit.
          part **a**: from the $Zn^{2+}$/Zn half-cell to the $Ag^+$/Ag half-cell
          part **b**: from the $Cu^{2+}$/Cu half-cell to the $Fe^{3+}$/$Fe^{2+}$ half-cell
          part **c**: from the $Cr^{3+}$/Cr half-cell to the $Cl_2$/$Cl^-$ half-cell
          part **d**: from the $Mn^{2+}$/Mn half-cell to the $Pb^{2+}$/Pb half-cell.

**2.14 a** (i) $E$ = more than $1.33\,V$

(ii) $E$ = less than $1.33\,V$

(iii) $E$ = less than $1.33\,V$

**b** (i) stronger oxidising agent

(ii) weaker oxidising agent

(iii) weaker oxidising agent

**c** high concentration $Cr_2O_7^{2-}$, high concentration $H^+$, low concentration $Cr^{3+}$

**d** Increasing the concentrations of reactants forces equilibrium to shift to the right in order to reduce these concentrations. Therefore, $E$ goes up and the $Cr_2O_7^{2-}/H^+$ solution becomes a stronger oxidising agent.

**2.15** $E^{\circ}$-based predictions refer to standard conditions, but lab conditions are not usually standard. (However, if the $E^{\circ}$ values for the two half-equations differ by more than $0.30\,volts$, $E^{\circ}$-based predictions are usually correct.)

$E^{\circ}$ values may predict that a reaction will occur, even though in reality the reaction may have such a slow rate that it is not observed.

**2.16** Add a catalyst; increase temperature; increase concentration of dissolved reactants; increase pressure of gaseous reactants; increase surface area of solid reactants.

# Chapter 3

**3.1 a** A central positive ion with one or more ligand species datively bonded to it.

**b** An atom, neutral molecule or negative ion which is able to use one or more lone-pairs to bond datively to a positive ion.

**c** A ligand with more than one lone-pair which can form more than one dative bond to a positive ion.

**3.2 a** The number of dative bonds formed between the ligands and the central positive ion in a complex ion.

**b** (i) 6

(ii) 4

(iii) 6

(iv) 4

**c** (i) 3+

(ii) 2+

(iii) 3+

(iv) 3+

**3.3**

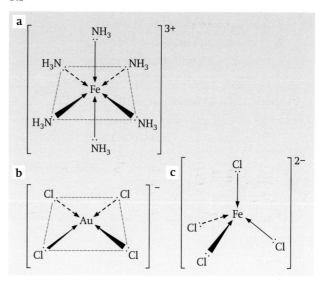

**3.4**

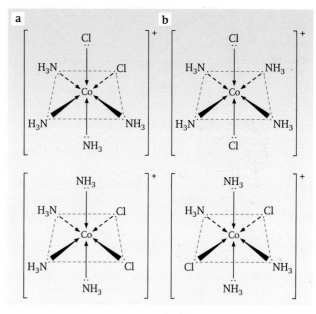

**3.5 a** The *trans* isomer is isomer 3

**b** optical

**c**

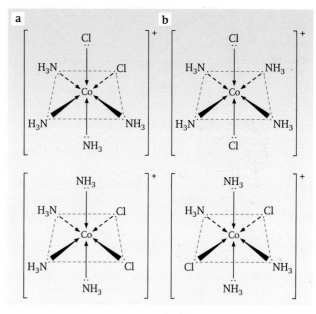

**d** $Co^{2+}$

# Chapter 4

**4.1** **a** It absorbs all visible light except blue.

**b** It absorbs all visible light except green.

**c** It absorbs all visible light except yellow (i.e. except green and red; it absorbs blue).

**4.2** **a–d** See *figure*.

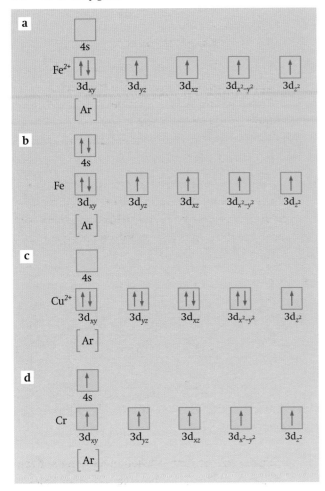

You will notice that in transition metal ions, e.g. $Cu^{2+}$ and $Fe^{2+}$, there are no electrons in the 4s orbital, but in transition metal atoms there are two electrons in the 4s orbital except for Cr and Cu which only have one. This gives rise to the surprising answer that both Cr and $Fe^{2+}$ have 24 electrons, but have different electronic configurations (see *Chemistry 2*, chapter 11 for an explanation of how 4s electrons are lost before 3d electrons during ionisation).

**4.3** **a** (i) Two of the 3d orbitals become of higher energy than the other three.

(ii) The size of the energy gap between the higher and lower energy 3d orbitals.

**b** The ligands cause d-orbital splitting by forming bonds along the axes of the $3d_{x^2-y^2}$ and $3d_{z^2}$ orbitals.

**4.4** **a** Moving from a lower energy 3d orbital to a higher energy one.

**b** The electron must absorb exactly enough energy for this promotion. Different colours of light deliver energy in different, exact, amounts.

**c** It is reflected/transmitted. This is the light we see.

**4.5** **a and b**
(i) no; $Cu^+$ is $3d^{10}$
(ii) yes
(iii) yes
(iv) no; $Ti^{4+}$ is $3d^0$
(v) no; $Zn^{2+}$ is $3d^{10}$
(vi) yes
(vii) yes
(viii) yes; the anion is coloured.

**4.6** **a** $[Fe(H_2O)_6]^{3+} + 6CN^- \rightleftharpoons [Fe(CN)_6]^{3-} + 6H_2O$

**b** $[Fe(H_2O)_6]^{2+} + 6CN^- \rightleftharpoons [Fe(CN)_6]^{4-} + 6H_2O$

**c** $[Ni(H_2O)_6]^{2+} + 3en \rightleftharpoons [Ni(en)_3]^{2+} + 6H_2O$

**4.7** The substitutions in the phthalocyanine molecule must affect its strength as a ligand, therefore changing the size of the $\Delta E$ of the copper ion and so changing which of the colours in visible light is absorbed by the complex.

**4.8** **a** Magenta or purple or violet, since it absorbs in the green and yellow regions.

**b** Red, since it absorbs in the violet, blue and green regions.

**c** Green, since it absorbs in the violet, blue and red regions.

**d** Magenta or violet, rather like part **a**, which has similar absorption in the green and yellow regions, but with a bit more blue.

# Chapter 5

**5.1** **a** Element is oxidation state 0, by definition.

$V^{2+}$ so oxidation state is +2.

$V^{3+}$ so oxidation state is +3.

$VO^{2+}$: V + (−2) = +2, so oxidation state is +4.

$VO_2^+$: V + 2(−2) = −1, so oxidation state is +5.

**b** Do you still know the colours?

**5.2** **a** $Zn + 2VO_2^+ + 4H^+ \rightarrow 2VO^{2+} + Zn^{2+} + 2H_2O$
The reaction occurs because the $E^\ominus$ for $VO_2^+/VO^{2+}$ is more positive than the $E^\ominus$ for $Zn^{2+}/Zn$, so Zn supplies electrons to $VO_2^+$.
(or $E^\ominus_{cell} = +1.76\,V$; the reaction occurs since $E^\ominus_{cell}$ is positive.)

**b** $Zn + 2VO^{2+} + 4H^+ \rightarrow 2V^{3+} + Zn^{2+} + 2H_2O$
The reaction occurs because the $E^\ominus$ for $VO^{2+}/V^{3+}$ is more positive than the $E^\ominus$ for $Zn^{2+}/Zn$, so Zn supplies electrons to $VO^{2+}$.
(or $E^\ominus_{cell} = +1.10\,V$; the reaction occurs since $E^\ominus_{cell}$ is positive.)

**c** $Zn + 2V^{3+} \rightarrow 2V^{2+} + Zn^{2+}$
The reaction occurs because the $E^\ominus$ for $V^{3+}/V^{2+}$ is more positive than the $E^\ominus$ for $Zn^{2+}/Zn$, so Zn supplies electrons to $V^{3+}$.
(or $E^\ominus_{cell} = +0.50\,V$; the reaction occurs since $E^\ominus_{cell}$ is positive.)

**5.3** The $E^\ominus$ for $V^{2+}/V$ is not more positive than the $E^\ominus$ for $Zn^{2+}/Zn$, so Zn will not supply electrons to $V^{2+}$.
(or $E^\ominus_{cell} = -0.44\,V$; the reaction does not occur since $E^\ominus_{cell}$ is negative.)

**5.4** $V^{2+}$ is oxidised to $V^{3+}$. The $E^\ominus$ for $Fe^{3+}/Fe^{2+}$ is more positive than the $E^\ominus$ for $V^{3+}/V^{2+}$, so $V^{2+}$ supplies electrons to $Fe^{3+}$, reducing it.
(or $E^\ominus_{cell} = +1.03\,V$; the reaction occurs since $E^\ominus_{cell}$ is positive.)
$V^{3+}$ is then oxidised to $VO^{2+}$. The $E^\ominus$ for $Fe^{3+}/Fe^{2+}$ is more positive than the $E^\ominus$ for $VO^{2+}/V^{3+}$, so $V^{3+}$ supplies electrons to $Fe^{3+}$, reducing it.
(or $E^\ominus_{cell} = +0.43\,V$; the reaction occurs since $E^\ominus_{cell}$ is positive.)
$VO^{2+}$ is not further oxidised to $VO_2^+$. The $E^\ominus$ for $Fe^{3+}/Fe^{2+}$ is not more positive than the $E^\ominus$ for $VO_2^+/VO^{2+}$, so $VO_2^+$ will not supply electrons to $Fe^{3+}$.
(or $E^\ominus_{cell} = -0.23\,V$; the reaction does not occur since $E^\ominus_{cell}$ is negative.)
The final oxidation state of vanadium is +4 in $VO^{2+}$.

**5.5** $VO_2^+$ is reduced to $VO^{2+}$. The $E^\ominus$ for $VO_2^+/VO^{2+}$ is more positive than the $E^\ominus$ for $SO_4^{2-}/SO_2$, so $SO_2$ supplies electrons to $VO_2^+$, reducing it.
(or $E^\ominus_{cell} = +0.83\,V$; the reaction occurs since $E^\ominus$ cell is positive.)
$VO^{2+}$ is then reduced to $V^{3+}$. The $E^\ominus$ for $VO^{2+}/V^{3+}$ is more positive than the $E^\ominus$ for $SO_4^{2-}/SO_2$, so $SO_2$ supplies electrons to $VO^{2+}$, reducing it.
(or $E^\ominus_{cell} = +0.17\,V$; the reaction occurs since $E^\ominus_{cell}$ is positive.)

$V^{3+}$ is not further reduced to $V^{2+}$ since the $E^\ominus$ for $V^{3+}/V^{2+}$ is not more positive than the $E^\ominus$ for $SO_4^{2-}/SO_2$, so $SO_2$ will not supply electrons to $V^{3+}$.
(or $E^\ominus_{cell} = -0.43\,V$; the reaction does not occur since $E^\ominus_{cell}$ is negative.)
The final oxidation state of vanadium is +3 in $V^{3+}$.

**5.6** **a** (i) $S + O_2 \rightarrow SO_2$
(ii) $SO_3 + H_2O \rightarrow H_2SO_4$

**b** First step: $SO_2$ oxidised, $V^{5+}$ reduced
Second step: $V^{4+}$ oxidised, $\frac{1}{2}O_2$ reduced

**c** Transition metals form stable compounds in more than one oxidation state.

**d** The catalyst provides an alternative pathway of lower activation energy.

**5.7** Adding $H^+$ (a product) forces the equilibrium to the left in order to remove the extra $H^+$ added. Adding $OH^-$ removes $H^+$ (a product) and forces the equilibrium to the right in order to replace the $H^+$ removed.

**5.8** **a** 6
**b** octahedral

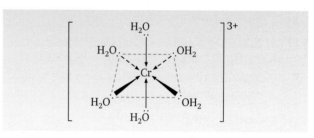

**c** Ligand substitution is when one or more of the ligands (in this case one or more water molecules) is replaced by a different ligand. This changes the size of the d-orbital splitting ($\Delta E$) of the $Cr^{3+}$; this changes the colour of the light absorbed and so changes the colour of the light we see.

**d** The violet $Cr^{3+}$ complex will have an absorption spectrum similar to that in figure 4.15 – it absorbs green.
The green $Cr^{3+}$ complex will have an absorption spectrum similar to that in figure 4.17 – it absorbs red and blue.

**5.9**  **a** ethanol

  **b** dichromate ions

  **c** Dichromate ions need $H^+$ ions in order to act as an oxidising agent.

  **d** $2Cr_2O_7^{2-} + 3C_2H_5OH + 16H^+$
    $\rightarrow 4Cr^{3+} + 3CH_3COOH + 11H_2O$

  ($2Cr_2O_7^{2-}$ will receive a total of 12 electrons, $3C_2H_5OH$ will supply a total of 12 electrons, hence $4Cr^{3+} + 3CH_3COOH$ in the products. Finally balance for $H^+$ and $H_2O$.)

**5.10**

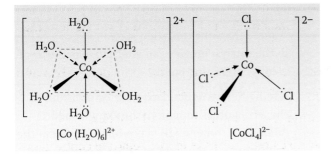

$[Co(H_2O)_6]^{2+}$ $\qquad$ $[CoCl_4]^{2-}$

**5.11**  **a** Pink to blue. Adding a reactant forces the equilibrium to the right.

  **b** Higher temperature forces equilibrium to the right in endothermic reactions.

**5.12**  **a** $2[Co(H_2O)_6]^{3+} + 2I^- \rightarrow 2[Co(H_2O)_6]^{2+} + I_2$

  **b** $[Co(H_2O)_6]^{3+} + Ag \rightarrow [Co(H_2O)_6]^{2+} + Ag^+$

  **c** $2[Co(NH_3)_6]^{3+} + Fe \rightarrow 2[Co(NH_3)_6]^{2+} + Fe^{2+}$

  **d** $[Co(NH_3)_6]^{3+} + V^{2+} \rightarrow [Co(NH_3)_6]^{2+} + V^{3+}$

**5.13**  **a**  (i) $[Ar]\ 3d^{10}\ 4s^1$

  (ii) $[Ar]\ 3d^9\ 4s^0$

  (iii) $[Ar]\ 3d^{10}\ 4s^0$

  **b** $Cu^{2+}$ compounds have an incomplete 3d sub-shell; if 3d is split d–d transitions are possible and certain colours of visible light will be absorbed. $Cu^+$ compounds have a complete 3d subshell, so no d–d transitions are possible and visible light will not be absorbed.

**5.14**  **a**

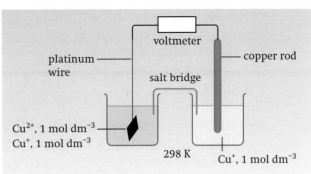

  **b** 0.37 V

  **c** the $Cu^+/Cu$ half-cell

  **d** $2Cu^+ \rightarrow Cu^{2+} + Cu$

**5.15**  **a** $Cu_2SO_4 \rightarrow Cu + CuSO_4$

  You would see a red-brown precipitate and a blue solution being produced.

  **b** Maintaining the concentration of $Cu^+$(aq) at $1.00\ mol\ dm^{-3}$ is a problem due to disproportionation.

**5.16**  The very poor solubility of CuI will mean the concentration of $Cu^+$(aq) will be extremely low. The concentration of $I_2$ is also low, particulary when the solutions are first mixed. This could result in:

  $Cu^{2+} + e^- \rightleftharpoons Cu^+$ $\qquad\qquad$ E = +0.40 V

  $\frac{1}{2}I_2 + e^- \rightleftharpoons I^-$ $\qquad\qquad$ E = +0.30 V

  This predicts that $I^-$ ions will reduce $Cu^{2+}$ ions.

**5.17**  **a** $\dfrac{47.8}{1000} \times 0.200 = 0.009\,56\ mol$

  **b** $0.009\,56\ mol$

  **c** $0.009\,56 \times 63.5 = 0.607\,06\ g$

  **d** $\dfrac{0.607\,06\ g}{1\ g} \times 100\% = 60.7\%$

  The final answer has been rounded to 3 significant figures as that is the accuracy of the data.

# Glossary

**bidentate** a bidentate ligand has two lone-pairs of electrons which can form two separate dative covalent bonds to a transition metal ion.

**complex ion** a transition metal ion bonded to one or more electron-donating species (ligands) by dative covalent bonds from the ligands to the metal.

**coordination number** the total number of dative covalent bonds from the ligands to the transition metal ion in a complex ion. Usually four or six.

**d-orbital splitting** the change that takes place in the d orbitals of a transition metal ion whereby two of the orbitals become of slightly different energy from the other three. This happens in complex ions.

**disproportionation** the oxidation and reduction of the same species in one chemical reaction.

**electrochemical cell** an exothermic chemical reaction set up as two half-cells in two separate containers so that the energy released can produce an electric current between them.

**electrode potential** the voltage measured for a half-cell. Another half-cell is essential for this measurement to be made.

**half-cell** half of an electrochemical cell. One half-cell supplies electrons, the other half-cell receives electrons.

**half-equation** describes what is happening in one half-cell. Alternatively, in a redox reaction a half-equation can be used to describe only the reduction reaction or only the oxidation reaction.

**isomers** differing forms of a compound or complex. Isomers have the same formula as each other but have differently shaped molecules.

**ligand** a species that can use one or more lone-pairs to form dative covalent bonds to a transition metal ion, forming a complex ion.

**ligand substitution (ligand displacement or ligand exchange)** the replacement of one or more of the ligands in a complex ion by different ligands.

**monodentate** a monodentate ligand can use one lone-pair of electrons to form one dative covalent bond to a transition metal ion.

**optical isomerism** a property of a complex whereby it can exist in two different shapes that are non-superimposable mirror images of each other.

**oxidation** the loss of electrons from an atom of an element, or from an atom or ion in a compound. Oxidation number goes up.

**oxidation state (oxidation number)** a number (with a positive or negative sign) assigned to the atoms of each element in an ion or compound. A positive oxidation number gives the number of electrons lost by the element on becoming part of the ion or compound; a negative oxidation number gives the number of electrons gained by the element on becoming part of the ion or compound. However, oxidation states are a useful tool rather than an infallible literal description.

**oxidising agent** a species that takes one or more electrons away from another species in a reaction.

**polydentate** a polydentate ligand has more than one lone-pair of electrons and can form more than one dative covalent bond to a transition metal ion.

**promotion** the movement of an electron from a lower energy orbital to a higher energy orbital. This requires the absorption of energy, often in the form of one colour of light.

**reducing agent** a species that donates one or more electrons to another species in a reaction.

**reduction** the gain of electrons by an atom of an element, or by an atom or ion in a compound. Oxidation number goes down.

**salt bridge** a piece of filter paper soaked in potassium nitrate solution used to make electrical contact between the half-cells in an electrochemical cell.

**standard conditions** a temperature of 298 K, all solutions at a concentration of $1 \, \text{mol dm}^{-3}$, all gases at a pressure of one atmosphere.

**standard electrode potential** the electrode potential of a half-cell when measured with a standard hydrogen electrode as the other half-cell. All conditions must be standard. If this value is negative the half-cell donates electrons to the standard hydrogen electrode. If this value is positive the half-cell receives electrons from the standard hydrogen electrode.

**standard hydrogen electrode** a half-cell in which hydrogen gas at a pressure of one atmosphere bubbles into a solution of $1 \, \text{mol dm}^{-3}$ $H^+$ ions. Electrical contact is made with a platinum wire. This half-cell is given a standard electrode potential of 0.00 V; all other standard electrode potentials are measured relative to it.

**standard reference electrode** a half-cell used as a standard – the electrode potentials of other half-cells can be measured relative to it.

**stereoisomers** compounds or ions with the same formulae but different shapes. The two types of stereoisomerism are geometrical or *cis–trans* isomerism (see page 24) and optical isomerism.

**transition element** a metal element that forms at least one ion with a partially filled d subshell. Not zinc or scandium.

**visible spectrometer** a device that separates the different frequencies of light from each other so that the presence or absence of particular frequencies can be noticed.